WINNING E-BRAND STRATEGIES

WINNING E-BRAND STRATEGIES

DEVELOPING YOUR ON-LINE BUSINESS PROFITABILITY

MARTIN BRIGHTY AND DEAN MARKHAM

First published in 2002 by
Spiro Press
17–19 Rochester Row
London SW1P 1LA
Telephone: +44 (0)870 400 1000

© M Brighty and D Markham, 2002

© Typographical arrangement, Spiro Press, 2002

ISBN 1 904298 540

British Library Cataloguing-in-Publication Data.
A catalogue record for this book is available from the British Library.

Library of Congress Cataloguing-in-Publication Data on file.

Spiro Press USA
3 Front Street
Suite 331
PO Box 338
Rollinsford NH 03869
USA

Typeset by: Concerto
Printed in Great Britain by: Cromwell Press
Cover image by: PhotoDisc
Cover design by: Cachet Creatives

To those who face up to the challenges regardless of criticism!

Martin Brighty

This work is dedicated to my father, who has given me the desire and motivation to succeed, and to my mother, who taught me that patience is a virtue for without that, I would never have been able to spend the many months putting this work together. Many thanks to you both for everything that you have instilled in me and for being there when I needed you.

Dean Markham

Contents

....

PART 4 TECHNIQUES USED IN WEBSITE OPTIMIZATION

Preface

Dean Markham, CEO of Search Engine Promotion Services (USA), and myself, Martin Brighty, a co-founder of Hunters, the branded men's silk tie maker (and operators of LuxuryTies.com), have written this book to give you a fresh insight into our world of e-commerce marketing techniques. Our aim is to help you make your website highly visible within the search engines and directories, thus increasing the numbers of visitors to your site, through the process of *optimization* – often referred to as search engine marketing.

Using a mix of brand development, marketing and technology, readers will come to understand the close relationship between these areas in an on-line environment, and how they can be deployed in a very simple way to create great site positioning results. Whether you are a business student, a business owner looking to get into e-commerce or a webmaster with a website that's never achieved very much – this book is for you.

Readers will be taken through an experience-based case study about Hunters and LuxuryTies.com, who found that just launching and submitting a website to the search engines wasn't going to be enough if they wanted to win business.

The process of optimization is complex and it can cost a small fortune to have an IT consultant do it for you – if you can optimize a website to perform high in the rankings or just understand how the process works you will be in the top 1% of all internet users!

To us *website optimization* is the process of creating a high-ranking website. Thus it is both a marketing and a technology tool, the ultimate aim being to generate site visitors through a managed process that converts into sales for your e-business.

Readers will learn how certain tactics can be utilized to enhance their knowledge in the area of site positioning, and will begin to understand other relevant concepts in branding that actually help you develop a website marketing process for your own e-commerce activity.

We have brought in some background material to give weight to our concepts, and in using Hunters/LuxuryTies as the case study, readers can relate this book to an event that has actually happened. This is not just a business book – it's a self-contained website marketing development and business module.

Introduction: marketing through generic term optimization

The whole concept behind the Hunters *www.luxuryties.com* website is, like all good ideas, fairly simple. It's the approach taken to development and marketing in e-commerce that differed from the rest of the market when we started designing our website back in September 1999.

Now we want to share with you the tips and tricks that we used to achieve the 'level playing field' (where businesses compete on equal terms) that was the popular talk among the media and business pundits – but from our own perspective as a small traditional British business with ambitions to sell our range of Savile Row silk ties around the world.

Importantly we want to dispel many of the new economy myths, in particular that only those with high marketing and advertising expenditure are absolute winners on-line.

Dean Markham and I worked closely optimizing LuxuryTies during the spring/summer of 2000. Together we developed a website marketing framework to support our Hunters' tie brand that would achieve the type of site visitors we wanted – focused traffic – using a technique that Dean has been at the leading edge of for some time out in California, the home of technology.

We (LuxuryTies) have won a lot of great search engine rankings using Dean's website optimization techniques which, when aligned with our own Hunters' niche brand development marketing programme, enabled us to mix the latest technology processes with some of the most established business practices.

Through Hunters' Inside UK Enterprises Host status (joint IUKE/DTI initiative) we meet many e-commerce enabled businesses that share a common goal: *they want their website returned within the top ten results for a generic product search term specific to what they have for sale.*

This book is based on data from the many presentations we give around the UK to businesses and students, and throughout you will see our slides with supporting background analysis, explaining and examining how we managed to use the process of optimization to develop the Hunters' brand position on-line.

The general function of optimization

One of the most telling comments we heard on the subject of search engine rankings was 'if you are not in the top ten results *you* [your website/company] aren't any good'. Indeed, how many people go beyond the first ten results returned to them by the search engine before clicking on one of those results or performing another search using a different word or phrase?

If you are not in the top results set returned you lose an opportunity. But what would happen if you were among the top ten results, comprised mostly of the big names/brands, those guys who spend millions on advertising and promotion, employing vast armies of marketing and ad agency executives?

We'd say you have done very well. If you get the customer you're taking business away from the big names, and as you are ranked with them, in the eyes of your browser or the web searcher, you are every bit as good as them – the only difference is that you are getting the customer for nothing!

Here's another way to think about optimization. Let's say you operate a website that hasn't been optimized and has a competitor base of 500,000 other websites selling or promoting the same product or service – eg shoelaces.

A browser types into the search engine search box 'shoelaces' and receives back the top results for the search which also states there are 500,000 other related sites.

Your site is in the results returned but your site is on page 50,000 – what chance have you got that the searcher will find you? Hardly any!

Now if you were in the first ten search results returned the odds of you being selected go down (depending on the engine you are using) to 10 to 1. What would you rather be – a rank outsider or a near favourite?

In a brand marketing exercise just being seen alongside the 'household names' pays dividends – you are a constant threat and in many ways you are cashing in on the market they have spent money developing.

Now that's what we call a level playing field.

Land grabbin' as an alternative

A great term we came across to get websites into a global marketing pattern was 'land-grab'. This one we really like, as many a dotcom start-up with their venture capitalists' (VC) money went hell for leather promoting their new e-business, buying expensive media and achieving what? – nothing, except some wild case studies at the business schools on how to burn through unimaginable sums of money!

In fact the only real winners were the advertising and marketing guys, who convinced the start-up that they needed to spend millions to win market share in markets that never really existed for the dotcom start-up's revolutionary, life-changing product or service in the first place.

One organization we read about blew $100 million in a year but generated only $40,000 in sales. Where's the managerial skill in that? We agree with the excuse they gave when they were forced to close down: 'the market wasn't yet ready for us'. But what an expensive way to find out!

So you didn't get those VC millions to blow on an ad campaign!

Many traditional businesses or new economy businesses base their business plan on existing/mature markets using e-commerce as either a corporate spin-off or to create some new means of adding value for the consumer's benefit.

When we meet with organizations that have realistic business plans we always find it hard to understand why they haven't managed to get funding. Maybe it's because they didn't try and trick a venture capitalist into parting with millions of pounds when it was difficult to justify £1 billion sales three years from start-up, or maybe the start-up was too honest about its market and the prospects of engaging a large multicultural global customer base. In either case we think they would have saved themselves a lot of trouble if *truth* had been the basis of their business plan.

Today the NASDAQ (the US technology stock market) and many other stock markets are littered with new media plc organizations that haven't made the grade and the list just keeps growing. About the only thing that will save many e-businesses before their cash runs out is if they are taken over (consolidated) by a bigger traditional business – the reverse of what the highly promoted and funded dotcom was set up for in the first place.

This book is for those (like us) who didn't get the funding, but still wanted to make their dream a reality. We have done just about everything possible to bring ourselves this far without an outside backer. If we did it, so can you.

These days as we look back, being on-line has been (and still is) a highly rewarding and valuable experience. We have learnt so much and met so many people. We have a fantastic on-line customer base, and we have received so much press that we have done better than many of the funded dotcoms – in relation to the $100 million US company mentioned earlier, our on-line sales in the first year were three times higher than theirs for 0.008% of their VC's investment!

Because we optimized for our customers and knew how to create a brand, the market was ready for us!

Footnote

Before you dive straight into the case study, here are some facts/thoughts to bear in mind as you review this text:

- The average cost of building a brand in today's market is $1 billion (source: Gary Hamel and C K Prahalad, *Competing for the Future*, USA/London: Harvard Business School Publishing, 1994).

- The average on-line cost of winning a new customer (acquisition cost) is $89.00. We calculated the value of our customer base and were very happy, as our customers had found us through our optimization techniques for nothing!

- When talking about their brand a famous perfume producer is said to have remarked: 'in the factory we mix chemicals, and on the shop floor we sell dreams' – which just shows what you can do with a chemistry set, a picture of a tropical beach and a nice bottle!

How this book works

Divided into four parts, it begins with a study on where Hunters was and where it wanted to be through its LuxuryTies website and e-commerce brand development programme. We analyze certain issues that are important in creating a segmented niche marketing campaign and, with our objectives set, we turn to the technology and search engine marketing expert (Dean Markham) and look for the how-to answers that you will be able to follow for your own business/on-line activity.

We then select a segment (or niche) of Hunters' overall market and optimize a home page to this market, showing you how to do it for yourself – or at least giving you an idea of what to tell your own web design/building team. This will enable you to meet your market head on and thus win the visitors that are actively searching for what you sell or produce.

Ultimately, through the product or service you have available, website visitors will be converted into sales. But that's your part – while we can show you how to generate and increase your website traffic, the lesson is that the market has to 'be ready for you' if they are to buy what you have on offer.

Life is all about self-help, which is what this book delivers. It will enable you to focus on a segment of your total market and create value through a programme of brand evolution and tactical e-commerce development, utilizing your own virtual organizational structure to its fullest. By the end of this book you will know what we know and will be able to apply the concepts we describe here and have already employed.

Importantly, you don't have to be an IT specialist or a business school graduate to do any of this. You just need to know that a system exists, and where and how that system should be used within your organization's value chain.

Getting started

The name of the game is winning sales but there's a lot of competition out there. We are always surprised that whenever we ask business schools or businesses how many have ever heard of the term 'optimization' we get about three hands raised out of thirty people, and yet it's the key to success!

You are about to embark on what was the biggest 'lesson' we learned in e-commerce – a lesson that led to a fundamental rethinking of our own marketing and brand development programmes. Like all really great concepts, it's not that difficult to understand providing you take the time to read and think about where and how you can apply this process.

So for those who had the great ideas but didn't get the VCs to buy in, here you are. This is your chance to make it happen now and show the world you can do it without anyone else's money.

The concepts surrounding the Hunters' tie brand

The steps and ideas that we describe in the Hunters LuxuryTies case study are summarised here as:

1. Gaining an intimate knowledge of your market.

2. Understanding how to generate added value.

3. Evaluating and selecting markets.

4. Brand definition for your segment.

5. Creating innovation in technology – understanding what applies.

6. Developing the distribution channel.

7. Using distinctive capabilities in brand development.

8. Updating and site content refreshing.

9. Becoming your market's authority.

10. Continual optimization to meet new market segments and niches.

To achieve this we will be working with a mix of case study and experienced-based analysis, supported with an actual optimization process that you will be able to follow.

About the authors

Martin Brighty MBA (Kingston University) and David Walker co-founded Hunters Partnership Ltd, the London Savile Row silk tie maker, in 1996, with £1,000 following redundancy. They have gone on to create a business that has been reviewed by many of the world's leading media, appearing in the *New York Times* and featuring on Sky News, for their website LuxuryTies.com and their range of ties.

Martin and David regularly appear as guest speakers to both business people and students of business alike, and Hunters is a host Inside UK Enterprise company, and was a finalist for Exporter of the Year (SME) 1998.

Martin Brighty may be contacted at:

info@luxuryties.com

Dean Markham is President/CEO of Search Engine Promotion Services established in 1999 and based in California. The company provides website marketing/promotion services, consulting and self-study manuals (available from their many different websites: www.search-engine-promotion-services.com, www.affordable-website-promotion.com and www.websurfer-netcafe.com) to a global audience eager to learn how to improve their e-business potential.

Previously Dean was facilitator and developer for a number of on-line workshops with a US-based training company, where he delivered workshops on 'Learning WebPosition Gold Software' and 'Search Engine Strategies and Techniques'.

PART 1

Getting to grips with e-commerce

CHAPTER 1

Starting out

Company and market background

Originally we couldn't afford to buy stock when we started Hunters, so we worked for companies who paid us in silk instead of money. The idea being that at least we would have something to show customers, which we could deliver immediately. Figure 1.1 gives an overview of the Hunters' background.

 Hunters – Savile Row, W1

* Luxury brand accessory producer – est. 1996

* Operating in global US$70 billion market

* B2B/B2C virtual structure business model

* World 'first mover' advantage – high media

* IUKE host member – e-branding/development

Figure 1.1 Hunters: basic background information.

The Hunters' 'version' of the new economy

The advent of the internet boom led us to believe that as soon as we created a site and went on-line we would win sales from all over the world – and that's what we really needed, especially after the way we started up.

Like so many others we bought into that thought process, which spawned a culture of entrepreneurialism here in Europe similar to that of the Klondike gold rush! Everyone we met had a great e-business idea, and they were pursuing their instant rags-to-riches dream with a steely determination.

The classic route for the new media entrepreneurs was the following:

- Have a really weird business idea while on the way home from the pub.

- Register a domain name – the wackier the better.

- Slap together a business plan that promised big markets as no one in the world could do without this new business, working on the assumption that the current market was already worth £10 billion and in the first year the new e-business would get a minimum 1% market share, through land-grabbing advertising.

- Twist investors to get their first 'hit' to pilot and soft launch the e-business, knowing that the investors don't understand the internet, and convince the gullible VC that four other investors are also looking seriously at the plan, and if they don't get involved now chances are it will be more expensive for them later on.

- Six months following the first 'hit' go back to the investors for the second round of funding once it has been proved that the management team have been able to meet the really testing milestone imposed by the investor, this normally being to build the website on budget (that's difficult). Spend the next load of money on 'developing the business model' meaning advertising and employing a lot of people wearing chinos, trainers and grubby t-shirts.

- Finally (about 12 months later) float the e-business following a real 'talking-up' by the investors' own PR people, selling the investors' (plus a big chunk of the original founders') shares to cash everyone out, while dumping the stocks on the market, to be quietly forgotten about while everyone who was once involved moves on to pastures new!

The sucker – the investor in the street who believed the share prospectus – is the one left holding the baby, which in this case is a load of worthless stocks that are never going to recover, let alone make a dividend payment.

Who won? Well, it looks like the venture capitalists could never lose because they controlled the run-up to the floatation. Neither could the founding management as they cashed out and were all part of the VCs' master plan to make more money.

On the basis of this route to riches it seemed easy, with not a mention of customers anywhere. In fact some of the new e-businesses didn't even have to generate a single customer to get their funding, everyone was going so dotcom mad.

But for many of us it was difficult to understand what the newly launched and funded e-business was all about in the first place and just how it was going to change lives. The question I would ask myself as I read through the financial pages (in a vain bid to work out how to gain investment) was how could a business run by people who had never been in business before suddenly warrant £10 million worth of VC money?

Then one day it came to me, like a blinding flash of inspiration. It actually didn't matter if these e-businesses didn't make it, providing the stock market stayed on a high. All of an investor's money would be recovered when the shares were floated, and most of the investors would talk up their target investee stocks knowing that the 'word, tip or nod' would get back to the fund managers. Then they (the VCs) were safe when they floated-off, as the new issue would be fully subscribed.

Capital markets such as the stock market are inefficient – they rely on information, just as business people do, to assess risk and return. However, it's the manipulation of the information and its subsequent ambiguity (along with who is on the distribution list) that allows the downside risk to be ignored to concentrate on the upside rewards.

In normal business circles there is a checking process called due diligence undertaken by accountants and regulated by statutory authorities. However, due diligence relies on the fact that there is some information to check, and as new businesses they didn't have any information that could be checked.

But this wasn't a problem to a VC and e-business as the investors made do with what information was verifiable. To supplement the lack of credible information the investors were careful to bring in a few 'household' business people to add weight to the business plan, giving the VCs a bit more confidence that the new business would meet the stock market criteria, beefing up the prospectus and so guaranteeing the float. It's a case of reputation, reputation and ignorance!

One business we got the 'word' on had, following a £7 million investment, managed to create a business with a whopping £177,000 per year turnover, which was enough to justify its float for a £700 million price tag (if they are reading this they'll know who they are, and so will the investor team behind them!) employing this criterion alone.

All this should lead you to consider that the biggest risk facing the funded dotcom was whether the stock market would suddenly wake up – which as history shows it normally does. All it takes is for someone to notice that a new media company with a £150 million investment just made their third £50 million loss on the quarter and has now revised its profitability forecast from the year 2002 to 2050. It's only then that fund managers go through their tech portfolio to check up on their other investments.

When this happened the problems really set in as the easy VC money dried up overnight, and all these new media entrepreneurs and old economy CEOs realized that their worst nightmare was about to come true – they were going to have to run their business and create money through customers (a new concept to many of them), and not through the investors' cash and the stock markets.

But as always there were more problems (as nightmares generally tend to only get worse): many of the CEOs at these new e-coms were ex corporate guys who were just not used to running new fast-paced businesses, which is why all these start-ups were gigantic rather than the normal small start-up types that we usually come across.

These CEOs couldn't start small – they had reputations, they wanted to start big and get even bigger. And as everyone knows, cash can do a lot – which is why they spent money on building what they called 'a business' but what we call 'a joke'.

Mostly, these CEOs had never gone near a customer in their entire career. They were generally frightened of customers as they always regarded the customer as being beneath them. Thus the ex big company CEO was like a fish out of water, without the security of the rows of middle managers in front of them to fend off problems. Suddenly they were going to have to work through the problems – they were in the thick of it.

We once heard someone say that if you wanted to run a small business you should buy a big one and be patient. Now most of those CEOs (if they've stuck around after their share options have hit the floor) have the great opportunity to try and run an on-line small business – if they can.

As we come to the end of our version of a short period in business history, the following (adapted) phrase comes to mind:

Never has so much been spent, by so many, to achieve so little!!

Hunters and the new economy

In retrospect as we started out with our e-commerce LuxuryTies programme our main advantage was that we had been a start-up before and knew the problems of winning business from all over the world when you are a new company. We had also already learned that a business needs an edge to beat the established and the new competitors.

What the hype didn't tell the dotcom entrepreneurs who formed new economy or new media companies operating with a single on-line sales mechanism, was that the majority of them had no chance, regardless of how much capital they had behind them.

Why? Because most of their companies were unknown, untried, untested and advertising *don't buy loyalty*.

Consumers like a reputation, a track record. No one likes anything new, especially when it's 5,000 miles away and asking for your credit card details for products you can't physically inspect or have any experience of beforehand.

People have no way of checking out the unknown organizations behind the fancy, heavy-saturation advertising. With so many start-ups coming along all at once it became difficult to cut through the pollution and din being generated by them, especially as they were all vying for the same customers with the same type of message.

Today so many websites just don't win any business or even achieve any visitors because they do not possess the reputation that being a brand delivers. They are not seen in the right places and, importantly, the sites don't say the right things to their target audiences.

As they are not established brands the website organizations have no endorsement of what they are about. Fundamentally they either tried, or are still trying, to establish themselves the quick way, thinking a mix of marketing and advertising is all it's going to take.

At Hunters we always knew what a true brand really is and how it is created. We know that a brand is its market leader through its inspiration, carved out in a niche market over time and endorsed by the customers and the media alike for its product and innovation which gives the customer the confidence to buy.

We did what so many other start-up and internet companies failed to recognize as key in the development frame: we focused on who our customers were and then defined and devised the technology around them to deliver a brand proposition through a unique mix of technology and segmented brand design.

Hunters – the origins

Hunters Partnership Ltd was formed during August 1996. It is a men's silk tie maker based in London W1 started up with £1,000 following our (Martin Brighty and David Walker's) redundancy from another established London tie-maker.

We decided to position our ties at the top end of the market in terms of quality as that was the market segment we had been 'brought up in' by our ex-employer. However, this choice of market position, in the pre e-commerce days, limited us to the major cities and towns in the few areas we could manage efficiently.

With so little money when we formed Hunters, life was very tough. Like all start-ups we had the dream, the enthusiasm and the energy, and with these alone one month later, in September 1996, we made our first sales trip to New York's Manhattan – our rationale being that there were more big stores there than anywhere else that could support a tie at retail in our price range.

We set about organizing the trip, booking two of the cheapest airline seats known to mankind. Arriving on a Friday at 6 pm local time and after a long coach ride out of JFK we found and checked into a one-bedroom downtown hotel (we have the coach driver to thank here for his recommendation) and a room the size of a handkerchief.

The first memory I have of New York is seeing the Manhattan skyline while crossing the Queensboro Bridge and recognizing all the famous landmarks – the Empire State Building, the Chrysler and City Corps buildings. Then, as you cross the bridge with these on your left, you are suddenly in the hustle and bustle of mid-town Manhattan.

I was so excited – early evening Manhattan, and I'm there on business.

Staring out of the windows as the coach bounced over the craters that tend to make up the NY roads, I was mesmerized – the big cars, the millions of yellow taxis and the sound of all the car horns blaring away, the sheer physical size of the skyscrapers and the people rushing around on their way about town.

When I got off the coach, the noise was intense. People were shouting around me and the heat of the place hit me straight in the face like someone had turned on a hairdryer. This was the New York I had dreamed of seeing all my life, and here I was, wide eyed and excited.

We had hardly any money and could only just afford a single room at the hotel. After checking in we had the idea that whoever won the most orders got to have the bed that night: the day's loser would have to sleep on the floor – what we call management by incentive!

Late into the night and early into the morning of that first weekend, we were busy in our room sticking clippings of our silk (that we had been paid in earlier) to home-made Hunters' headed design cards. When Monday finally arrived we took our new design cards round to the buyers in a blitz on the major stores, phoning from call boxes for appointments (not daring to run up the hotel bill), and waiting for ages in receptions with the hope that when the buyer said to come along if they got 'five' they would have a quick look and we would win an order.

In the weekday mornings we would go off in separate directions arranging to meet up later to assess how we were getting along, giving each other tips on what was in the stores and what the buyers told us they were looking for.

We were probably two of the poorest guys in the most vibrant and breath-taking city in the world. I don't think we even noticed just how little we had between us, but after that first week of frantic activity we had won £50,000 worth of orders, enough to start off properly, convince the bank we were serious and look for rented London W1 premises from which to operate Hunters.

If anything, we both remember the excitement like it was yesterday, even the holes in our shoes didn't seem so bad (the weather stayed fine all week). I am sure we were two of the proudest people walking out of Heathrow airport the following Saturday morning as we had won orders in the greatest city in the world – it was the most magical feeling and the best start we could have hoped for.

When we got back home, we organized a quality workforce, made up the silks for the US orders and started to make the first deliveries one month later – our first delivery was to a New Yorker for three metres of blue and white polka-dot silk material (and here we take the opportunity to say 'thank you' to Felix!).

To a lot of companies a £75 order would be nothing but to us it was everything, as we knew we could get more. It gave us the confidence boost we needed after two days of hearing 'come back in January' or 'I just placed my order with another company' to keep trying harder.

Although the orders we were being given were like the scraps or crumbs off the table they were fantastic for us and just enough for a small, untried and untested start-up which is always eager for any order, regardless of its size, in a bid to prove itself.

We have never turned business down to this day and never will as we remember when we had to fight to get our range in front of the store buyers. We had to make sure our service and quality was everything we said it was going to be if we were to win the important larger repeat business that credible established suppliers generate.

Today we never lose sight of the fact that our customers are the most important people in our business. Without them we are nothing. No order is too small or too big, and we remain grateful to and conscious of those who pay our wages.

From that first week in NYC we have never looked back. These days when we go on a sales trip we can have a room each and can eat in the hotel restaurant, but the sandwich from the deli still tastes every bit as good now as it did then, the view of the New York skyline still generates butterflies in our stomachs and our excitement and enthusiasm for what we do has never faltered regardless of the bad days we sometimes still have. We know that if we managed to survive and win in New York on £1,000, we can survive anything.

We suppose that if life was a game show the 'Hunters' Challenge' would read something like this:

> *Would you go to New York – the most competitive city in the world – as an untried and untested start-up with only £1,000 between two people and no guarantees of anything except that back home the mortgage needs paying and the family needs feeding?*

We don't even like reading that back to ourselves, but at the time it was the risk we took. We made Hunters work because we wanted it to and it had to.

Hunters and LuxuryTies.com

As we went on in business we were always aware that it was our retail customers who decided whether or not to stock our ties. If a retailer has its own favourite brands it is not going to add any new ones that are not supported by advertising, something we just didn't have the money for – and five years on that's pretty much still the case.

Just like a retailer, though, we always wanted to get nearer to our customer (our tie-wearing public). However, the option available to us before the internet was to set up a shop in a very select location, but for that you need money which is always in short supply within any small business.

We always knew there was more business around the world to be won but we lacked the funding to exploit the opportunities and couldn't even get a foothold to the extent that over time (five years plus) we might be able to develop a small market. It's no good making one sales trip each year when your customers need to see you three times.

To overcome the marketing shortfalls in our old b2b economy (the traditional business model) we used almost every free and subsidized UK government small business service to help us develop the US as our main export market, quite successfully.

Without their help the story would be very different today, which brings us to the issue we faced: why, if we had a relatively strong export market running alongside our domestic market, did Hunters need an internet b2c presence? There were two reasons:

- We could reach the global market – without physically having to travel all over the world – on a low budget and increase our sales.

- If we didn't get involved, we would miss the boat, and the new highly funded e-businesses were beginning to worry us.

Today we regard an internet presence as vital. Our product is small, is understood by its market and is ideal for dispatch by courier/postal services – basically it was made for the internet!

Many organizations on the wholesale/manufacturing supply side are now bypassing existing channels of distribution, such as Hunters and its retailers, and going direct to the final purchaser. New organizations (e-businesses) are being created continually just to sell ties and men's accessories, some winning the funding to achieve a sustainable business model in what is a highly profitable global market for those who can get it right.

The site www.luxuryties.com was the result of a number of business development factors. Initially they were all commercial, but once the project to create a Hunters' web presence was underway our attitudes changed. In the end our objective was to see if we could replicate the elements of an actual shopping experience on-line, and create a website that would be both enjoyable and innovative.

What we didn't fully appreciate was how the internet actually worked. Like so many others we thought you built a website, launched it and waited for the sales to roll in – instant riches. How wrong we were!

In fact we couldn't have been more off target if we'd tried, as the internet is about technology and the use of that technology within a marketing framework.

Our thoughts were that in designing a great website we would capture the imagination of all the 600 million daily tie wearers, which would lead to multimillion pound sales and our being 'consolidated' by a luxury brand house. Talk about ambition!

The problem was that as a traditional producer in a mature market we were not regarded as 'new economy' enough and were written off by many: 'Savile Row ties on-line – a nice idea, but it won't catch on. People will always want to buy their clothes in a store – touch is important when it comes to fabric.'

Returning to earth, we had to agree with that, but maybe on our travels we had found something that could replace this 'touch' purchase factor (explained later in this case study). In doing so we might win the confidence and trust of our market – enough to overcome this purchaser 'feel' factor – as we began to emerge as a brand, from whom people buy on the strength of reputation alone.

There are a couple of points to note at this stage. First, in competitor base terms, there are about 580,000 other e-businesses selling ties and related men's accessories. This continues to increase, and when off-line channels are added that total competitor base today numbers in the millions.

Secondly, at the time of the LuxuryTies website development we had (as usual) very little money to spend while most of the really serious players were investing heavily. In fact every day someone was winning vast sums of money to roll out the next generation of world-leading business.

In our view we had a sound product which had cut its teeth in the real world. Through us it was evolving as a brand as we had been marketing it since 1996, and with a little luck our 'fabric feel factor replacement' idea would catch on, although we had to replace luck with a workable business tactic. The trouble was that we had to find one, and then make it work on an almost non-existent budget.

The changing business landscape

SMEs can globalize if they choose to and we have met many SMEs that share our passion for the internet. Sadly, however, most go about it the wrong way and we could have easily made the same mistakes.

With the constant need to win new business, all organizations have to accept the fact that they now have to move outside their regular community using the internet and its technology as we did. The internet is not just a matter of checking prices between two like products; it's about creating and delivering engaging customer experiences that project your business into world markets.

The significance of this to an SME increases when, like us, their competitor base multiplies tenfold over a period of months, enabling price checking across continents for the same brand product and service propositions.

There's no point sitting back calling it a 'hype' or 'fad'. Such competition is here to stay as it is being driven by technology, making it totally different from any other kind of competition we have ever experienced. New variables are being brought into the business frame that we have no experience of but have to master in order to develop and keep up with our new competitors.

However, the real 'decider' was when we performed a generic term keyword search using the word 'ties'. We were astounded at the amount of competitors we suddenly had – 580,000, most of whom we had never heard of until then.

If the internet did anything for us at that stage in our business's life it was to scare us into action – and it was worth the fright.

CHAPTER 2

Creating an on-line sales channel

Through our b2b endeavours we had been invited to give a trunk show (where we take a steamer trunk to a store and display our ties as a special event) at the US Marine Corps HQ, Pentagon City, Washington DC (September 1999).

While we were there people were asking for our website address. We began by answering that we didn't have one, but in the end were saying one was being built to save our continued embarrassment!

We were originally invited by the people who managed the US Marines store, which is frequented by service personnel. Calling it a 'store' is doing it an injustice as the place itself is more like something you would find in Knightsbridge or on Fifth Avenue, an incredibly smart retailer and quite an experience for us as we met the kind of people you only ever read about in the newspapers or watch on CNN.

During our time there we were able (and I think for the first time) to observe people's buying habits in a natural shopping environment over a longer period. This led to the discovery of a feature of our market that even we, with our many years of experience, had overlooked.

Discovering the optimum on-line display feature

When we arrived at our designated part of the menswear department we initially just set up the ties on plain stands. After a while people started coming over just to hear us talk about our Savile Row ties.

Really, though, apart from the fact that there were a couple of 'English guys over by that tie stand', we just weren't generating a buzz among the shoppers. This was because, when we finished putting our tie display up and stood back to admire our handiwork, all we had was just a tie stand, among a lot of other tie stands (many of them the major brands). There was nothing to make our ties look any different from anyone else's.

As the day went by we talked to different people as they drifted around the store. However, we started to witness heated arguments between men and women who, on entering the store, had split up and gone off in different directions, one in search of a tie, the other in search of a shirt.

On their meeting back up – normally in front of us as the till was directly behind us – the male element of this search party would be told in no uncertain terms to put his proposed purchase back. The expert element of the team (the female) would then explain why what he had selected would look dreadful and would not match anything he already owned, despite his strongly 'suggesting' that it would!

At first we didn't take much notice but after this had happened quite a few times we began to realize how important matching shirts and ties were to Americans. We also discovered who was actually making the ultimate purchase decision – the female – and that this was based on the match between the tie and the shirt.

We had a chat among ourselves about this during our break and decided to test an idea. With the hope of increasing our own sales performance, we went around the store and at the shirt counter asked if we could borrow a few shirts on which to display some of our ties. Out of politeness more than anything else, the shirt concession manager agreed to lend us a few.

The response was amazing. People would stop and look, not bother to ask us anything and start making selections along with shirt/tie comparisons. The tills started ringing and our ties began selling – and we didn't witness another heated 'discussion' between male and female again, although we did get drawn into a few stand-offs but they were mostly light-hearted – we think!

Bringing an off-line key purchase criterion on-line

On the plane home from Washington DC we discussed our display methods. Clearly, mixing and matching shirts with ties was the way to sell on-line. So from September to November 1999 we began to look seriously at developing our existing e-mail ordering service (described later) into a website, drawing on the lifestyle data we had collected from our earlier attempts at direct sales.

Back in London our first step was to research other tie websites. By now we were not just thinking about sales but how we could take that main feature of a tie purchase decision and replicate it on-line, giving the customer their important purchasing criterion of *matching ties to shirts – without the arguments!*

Eventually we thought up a visual way that allowed people to select a tie and then change the background shirt to see how it would look against ten of the most popular colours/styles of men's shirts – to the point where we could actually interact with someone's own clothes. This was achieved with the aid of a database and some fairly smart technology that was already available but being used in non-clothing areas.

With the help and suggestion of our site builders, a Java Window – a platform-independent computer language used in developing internet applications – was created that would enable someone to upload a scanned image of their shirt on to our site and then put any of our ties on to their shirt image to check the match.

This provided real choice and selection capability. To interact with something someone already owns, anywhere in the world, 24 hours a day, 7 days a week, 365 days a year was to us quite remarkable, and we coined the phrase 'a bit of Savile Row in your front room'.

E-business planning – the focus

Business is full of surprises. In many instances the decisions you take are situation-based. Some work in favour of your plan, others against, but the real winners are ideas that you only get if you know your market well.

There are no tricks to beat the surprises. Planning is important, but fixed route plans get you nowhere – especially with this evolving technology that serves to increase your competitor base.

Although Hunters had a business plan when we started back in 1996, to look back at it today with hindsight shows just how much our markets have changed and how at best we were only half right. The internet doesn't even get a mention, although a lot of other wishful thinking does – most of which never happened.

That's because life has always been tough in the small business sector. Everyone is under the same pressure in terms of winning orders, cash-flow planning, debtors, creditors and everything else that goes with it. In the end you get into a routine and new development becomes impossible as you focus purely on the daily running of the business rather than its future growth.

Some people are lucky in their businesses – they hit on a real winner and fly. But for the vast majority it's a game of cat and mouse, thinking on your feet and spinning plates, so we at Hunters had to try and work out a way of using the internet to ease this pressure and actually do some development to break out of the routine that had set in. More often than not, however, it still felt like we were working at our old company doing the same thing, in the same way and for pretty much the same or worse results.

We found over time that the best plans are usually the ones where the goal is the focus and the route flexible. As we say, conditions change continually, and the only constant features are the pressures and the goals that we as business people set ourselves and which take up all our available time and resources.

Our views have evolved and today we believe that to rely completely on e-commerce as the main distribution mechanism is, and continues to prove, disastrous for many pure-play dotcoms. A number of these companies with cash flow left are moving into multiple distribution channels, combining off and on-line activities and rewriting their original plans that were presented to the VCs. Meanwhile the latter are all certain of making massive returns or holding bumper equity days, when their investee company's shares are cashed out on flotation.

While we agree that it makes commercial sense to have a business plan, for an unfunded SME it can only serve as an outline. More often than not time to reflect and craft one is in short supply and today we feel that the maximum effort in thought and writing should go on the brand building, marketing, customer focus and sales functions.

In an on-line environment, research into these elements alone dictates exactly with what and how you will tackle your market – it's great having a strategy but let's remember that a small business has too much to do already without crafting a Harvard-style business document in the hope of finding a venture partner. So, the concentration must be on customer focus, our maxim being 'sales equals cash flow' with the support message 'you don't make it, you don't spend it'.

One fact of life is that a business cannot just 'buy' loyal customers as if they are a commodity. Advertising doesn't fool anyone; if you can't see a use for a product/service in your life would you still buy it just because there's so much promotion around it?

The companies who have lost millions trying to convince customers that they couldn't do without a product or service should have thought longer about their customers' intelligence level and markets before they launched.

By now you should realize the name of the game is cash through sales. It's the route you take to achieving this that impacts upon the style and type of tactics you mix on-line to meet your (and your bank manager's) needs, and any development you undertake must be focused towards the sales goal.

CHAPTER 3

Developing an on-line business

Collecting market data

Before we even decided to develop www.luxuryties.com we were already testing alternative b2c direct sales approach methods by e-mail.

During the spring of 1999 we began discussing the need to increase our sales and margins through a direct final customer approach (b2c) when we saw a TV programme profiling a club with a number of members.

The following day we called them, in the hope that they would give us some PR in their newsletter and in return we would give their members a special discount on our ties. We supported this with a process that allowed members to order from us by e-mail, as the newsletter did not incorporate photographs.

We sent a lifestyle questionnaire to those who e-mailed us with an interest in buying a Savile Row tie, which they completed and returned. People told us what sort of job they did or which special event the tie was for. Following our assessment of their lifestyle we e-mailed back tie designs that we thought were suitable. To our amazement this process actually worked!

The success was really due to the design of the questionnaire (shown in Figure 3.1 overleaf). Initially we tested it on people to make sure it gave us the information we needed to make an appropriate selection of designs. Thus we started making our first (limited) b2c sales by e-mail.

Dear Sir or Madam

Thank you for your enquiry.

Hunters' ties are made from pure silk using only the highest quality weight fabrics in either woven brocade or printed Foulards and as such are work-room produced, being classical in cut to meet shirting and collar requirements (necktie specifications: 142 cm long by 9½ cm at the wide blade).

Ties are hand-slipped stitched, lined with pure wool and finished with silk topping to tone. Each tie has a self-keeper loop secured in the seam and is accompanied by our exclusive Hunting Horn marque brand name label.

To place details of your current requirement please complete the docket below, and return via e-mail or fax, and upon receipt a selection of the designs will be forwarded for your consideration.

Event	Colours	Design		Shirtings
Business/City Informal/Country Gift (Please indicate for type of wear)	Preferred or favourite colours Ground design	Abstract (bright colours/designs) Motif (animals/fruit/floral etc.) Contemporary (neat designs) Please indicate design type preferred		If you are hoping to match a particular shirt colour/stripe combination please detail as "main colour & stripes"
1.				
2.				
3.				
4.				
5.				

Please indicate preferences towards woven or printed ground silks.

Delivery
Will be by recorded post within five working days following receipt of your confirmation.
For neckwear required urgently a courier service can be arranged.

Costs
Neckties are sold individually at the current list price of £34.95 incl of VAT (plus postage and packing).
All accounts are sent out Friday of each week.
Thank you for taking time to complete the above, and a selection of tie designs will be e-mailed back to you for your consideration.
When ordering please provide us with your name, address, post code and telephone number to ensure a prompt response to your enquiry.

Figure 3.1 The Hunters' lifestyle questionnaire.

However, this was one of the hardest projects we ever undertook – we were selling a visual product on a lifestyle questionnaire. People told us so much about themselves that we began to create a profile of our customers' lifestyles. The results gave us a detailed insight into our final tie-wearing customers, ie the type of people who wear our ties and what additional factors beyond 'design and choice' were important to them in purchasing. The data also included information such as their profession, favourite colours, the peak buying times for new accessories, along with the colour of shirt they were trying to match the tie with.

This data proved invaluable when we came to develop and launch our website as we knew our markets intimately and could design our content (the written and visual elements of LuxuryTies) specifically to appeal to our target audience.

Armed with this customer analysis along with our new and radical way of presenting ties, life became very interesting. We knew we had the basis of a good idea, but the question was just how could we convey it to a global market?

Faced with that identified challenge we were again caught up with the same feelings of excitement we experienced when we first started Hunters. With so many other websites selling ties in such a plain and ordinary manner, a niche market had to exist for our brand of ties on-line, but it would be the communication of our great new technology breakthrough that would help us win through in our markets in the first place.

Looking at what was being spent on normal above- and below-the-line advertising (where above the line is, for example, TV advertising and below is the point-of-sale promotions that you see in stores, such as buy two get one free) by the big funded websites we also suffered a sense of angst. We knew that what we had designed would engage people but it was going to be impossible to market on a zero budget, especially with so many websites being promoted simultaneously. We could not figure out a way to overcome this.

However, we were so confident about our technology application that we just ignored the issue of a zero promotion budget and ploughed on regardless, sticking with another of our old off-line business mottos: 'it's your customers that make you – if they enjoy what you represent they'll buy'. Not many dotcoms ever realized that, they just went ahead and blew their VC's money.

To us LuxuryTies evolved as a new business venture, just like starting Hunters again with its late nights, worn shoe leather and stale sandwiches!

This time though we were able to go back to the drawing board, look at what we had previously created in our original business model, be very critical of ourselves and redesign the way we were going to work in the future. We just might do some business development that would break us out of our routine.

Process of website design – on-line analysis and training

With no 'big VC money' or experience of integrating e-commerce within an existing b2b traditional operation, we had to do the spadework outlined in Figure 3.2 ourselves. It took us over three months to find internet-based companies to whom we felt comfortable entrusting our website idea, and this was after we had telephoned, e-mailed and generally made nuisances of ourselves as we broke down the jargon barriers that the IT people have created for themselves.

 Interactive Interface!!

Designing a compelling e-commerce play:

✳ User experience – what they imagine it should be

✳ Technology identification

✳ Importance of purchase drivers

✳ Convince the market this is 'how it should be'

✳ Keep the clicks to purchase down to a maximum of 4

Figure 3.2 Developing an imaginative on-line play.

On top of this we must have looked at over 500 tie and related sites, learned what they could or could not do for their customer, and then worked out how we could create our site for under £5,000, leaving us a global marketing budget of £500 – a far cry from the 'land grab' theorists with millions to throw about. However, with a little improvisation, innovation, inspiration and – dare we say it – 'luck' we could just about do it as we had the customer-focused intelligence.

First, we needed to get some training to make up for our lack of e-knowledge while the site was going into construction. Our first point of call was a UK business support service called Business Link London, who were running a morning programme for £45 on aspects of e-commerce.

For three hours we watched and listened as an export development counsellor gave us an excellent overview of the challenge we were about to face and the pace of change within e-commerce itself.

We were absolutely amazed at what was presented and how the technology was being applied. Most importantly, we learned that it didn't matter if you were the smallest company in your sector – you could beat the biggest organizations. This was even more true in our market as everyone on-line was displaying ties in the same way, like a catalogue, whereas we had developed interactive protocols that would deliver an actual buying experience to the user/browser.

In short, we could compete with global funded organizations, and the result we achieved is the site you see today – a world first for its use of technology in the clothing b2c sector. We are the only interactive site in our class that enables uploading with something someone already owns, and remember that we are just two people in a very traditional/mature industry owning and operating a small business that must sell to survive.

With the site construction underway:

- we widened our research to include a review of all available on-line marketing methods, site requirements and business styles

- we spent a minimum of one hour a day for six months just looking at other sites and emerging technologies

- we carefully defined our market in terms of the ideal purchaser and why people would buy from us.

Our logic was that by the time our site was five days old we would be efficiently targeting, in a highly focused manner, as many of our profiled customer types as possible and we would be trained to a level that was competent for our new e-market.

Locating and addressing Hunters' primary internet goals and objectives

Organizations without large sums of investment money, would be surprised at what can be achieved by studying the customer and designing the site around them.

Originally we identified four areas central to the development of a website within our existing business, but clearly to categorize only four areas is too simplistic. However, the thought process we used is relevant when creating a broad framework with which to begin an e-commerce brand website development programme.

Also, four stages are easier to take in. We are not technical people, but we know how to sell, and we had learned what features of our product have an influence at the point of consumer purchase – today what we call browser/site viewer drivers.

The four stages we identified are summarized in Figure 3.3.

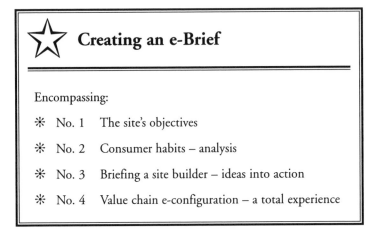

Figure 3.3 Four stages to creating an e-brief.

Stage 1 – The e-objective

Initially we wrote a one-page summary of the proposed site itself. The idea was to visualize where we wanted Hunters to be within an e-market environment and to decide which elements from our current product range (the designs) were in fact suitable for the web. With a visual product it is important only to show designs that will look good on-line and for a high-impact visual display it was regarded as paramount that we should only show those designs that were representative of Hunters' traditional Savile Row styling.

The written information and pictures are how we sell, so relevancy and consistency in our designs and company culture/ethics have to be available for checking by customers/browsers. All the supporting factual information on the company (location, our families' tailoring origins back in mid-18th century England) has to be verifiable, and backed up in a series of quick visual aids, such as the picture of the Savile Row street sign. All this then had to be encased in a short summary to validate our opening brand credentials, without trying to say too much about the ties themselves.

We found the simplest way was to examine our on-line competitors' offerings, and try to understand why they had created sites in the way they had and why they were showing ties in the way they were. Questions that had to be asked and answered were:

- What site features are the same? Are some items 'must have'? Would our credibility be damaged if we did not look or act like the others?

- What could we do better? Were there any elements that, even with our limited knowledge of technology, we could employ to enhance our site?

It was vital that we looked not only at sites that were relevant to the clothing sector from all over the net, but also at 'hot sites' from other sectors, noting which ones we liked and for what reason. In this way we could work out if any technologies being used elsewhere could be employed on our website to make it better than our competitors' one-dimensional displays – the use of a Java Window *applet* for example.

At this point readers should note that within our (and many other) website sales channel applications there are in fact two distinct types of business operating. Very early on we realized that our site must contain and achieve the following:

- an e-business element – where we present the information to our target audience, in a succinct and highly relevant manner

- an e-commerce element – where the customer pays or the transaction arises, which in our case is when the on-line order form is completed and the payment data entered.

Many organizations fail to make this distinction, which leads to the emphasis being skewed towards either one or the other aspect. We saw a number of sites that either had great style and poor purchasing information/ability, or the opposite – great paying techniques but poor content. Perhaps this depends on the management culture running your business. As is often the case, the finance director becomes responsible for the IT budget, and as finance is important to them, the money side is given priority.

We wanted to appear design orientated with a traditional quality product but with a technically advanced website. So the first thing we wanted was to simultaneously show our Savile Row brand credential and reveal what we could do for the tie browser/buyer that no other website in the same product class could. In short we wanted our on-line tie browser market to look upon our ties as they would view an expensive wristwatch from a high-class jeweller and imagine the ownership benefits.

However, as the confidence factor is also based on operating a secure payment system (it is equally as important to us as it is to our customers) our site builders created and placed payment/secure information, very conveniently, *after* the purchase choice has been made by a customer. Just like making a purchase in a store, the customer selects their goods and then pays. Many other sites get this backwards, through continuous bombardment with special savings and offers before a site visitor actually gets to see the product.

This total mapping process took us right back to and through our original value chain. We were concerned that e-business areas would not match our current business style and be difficult to integrate, as we were effectively promoting to a new and larger customer base while attempting to retain our existing b2b retail customers who may have felt we were indirectly competing with them. If you look at your own business, you may already sell direct to other businesses who perform some function that makes your product or service consumer ready. Hunters are a business to business (b2b) type company in the first place, and as such there would have to be changes, especially in the areas of customer support and stock management.

Financially the opportunity to 'go direct' is more viable for Hunters than staying solely in its existing value-added chain, as the more processes a silk tie goes through to arrive at the consumer the more value it attracts. We sell to the stores and these stores have a mark-up (in some instances up to 300% on their own purchase price from us). This added value includes distribution charges (freight), handling commissions, etc. We are at the start of this value-added chain and by the time Hunters' ties get on to the store shelves they end up looking very expensive in the eyes of our tie-wearing customers.

Our existing customers in the b2b environment also needed 'protecting' and therefore an e-tie design range had to be developed that was separate from our current wholesale range of designs. The last thing we wanted was the same tie design turning up in a retail customer's store when it was also available from us on-line.

This e-range is completely different from the range we show our retail customers. It has to be, to protect our retailers, as price comparatives arise both through on-line research and at base level. We wanted our on-line ties to be unique and not available anywhere else.

We had to evaluate ourselves not in terms of a b2b wholesaler but in terms of our ability to perform as a b2c retailer, untried and untested in a global, faster paced and highly competitive market, servicing individual website customers to the levels they would expect from a Savile Row outlet.

Stage 2 – Augmenting LuxuryTies to match consumers' existing habits

☆ Low Cost e-Start-up

I make the following recommendations:

　✳　Design the site yourself, create a mock up

　✳　Launch after tests on your target audience

　✳　Aim to develop the site over six months – refine

　✳　Work with a site builder you can pay in instalments

　✳　DON'T BUY OFF THE SHELF – bespoke wins!

Figure 3.4 Concepts of low cost start-up.

Again we carried out research to answer all our questions about how people would actually use an interactive tie site. Initially we had to create a mock website on paper, using photocopies of ties and shirts from magazines stuck down with Blu-Tack and tape. It was a real scrap-book effort but it enabled us to explain in very simple terms what we wanted LuxuryTies to do.

We produced all the written content and chose pictures based on the analysis of the lifestyle questionnaires we had received back from our e-mail sales earlier. This provided a focus on what is important to the tie buying public and how it should look through their eyes, not ours.

We set about testing the paper version of our website on friends and relatives until they all avoided us. We kept all this consumer testing data, and it is surprising as we look back now that, while some of our original ideas have remained, the site continued to move beyond our ambitions during building and as we kept upgrading our consumer research to narrow down the focus of the content to our target market users' subconscious codes.

Evolution is important. However, as we said earlier, while your goal should be cast in stone make sure the route to it is flexible, as the changing technology landscape continues to improve the way consumers see and evaluate information. If we look back, the technology we started with has been upgraded many times in just 12 months, and the next 12 months are going to be just as much of a challenge.

To meet the entire market and face up to the competitive landscape you must ensure your site has good updating facilities that are simple to employ and fairly low in cost. To remain the centre of attention through technological innovation on a zero budget is difficult. However, you would be surprised at what can be achieved by improvising, providing you keep the 'clicks to purchase' ratio down and don't bore your site user with non-relevant, go nowhere features, which you think are great but really don't live up to expectations or actual user needs.

Technology is continually dropping in price, and what was expensive 12 months ago is now cheaper. For LuxuryTies, it was how we were able to mix alternative dated technologies and repackage them into a new role that gave everything a new lease of life. The Java Window, for example, is a very old application used by opticians and in some hairdressers. It was our rewriting of what it was used for to meet our markets' needs – to help people scan in their own shirts and make sure they matched our ties before they purchased – that was new.

Stage 3 – Putting our ideas into action

Having gathered information, mostly from existing websites, and profiled site users, we made inquiries to locate a credible website builder. We could not find any company better than Internet Assist, who work for a wide range of organizations, large medium and small, producing quality bespoke websites – not off-the-shelf web packages which all look and work in the same way with the only difference being the products for sale. These latter sites remind us of cloned mail-order catalogues – our opinion is that anyone who buys one of these off-the-shelf websites doesn't care about the internet and will not engage their market.

Through working closely with Internet Assist, the final version of the LuxuryTies site was beyond what we had first conceived. They took our ideas and transformed them into what you see today, once described as a use of Interactive Interface Technology Protocols (Professor Raymond Burke, Kelly Business School, Indiana State University).

Creativity itself comes in many guises and those most guilty of lack of originality of thought are people who have never once had to think outside their own box. We made sure we only ever dealt with experienced people who were from a diverse range of backgrounds. If we couldn't find them we designed the experience for ourselves, then translated our ideas into a working brief for someone to follow.

The building process included the creation of a test site – an on-screen draft version of LuxuryTies that showed what we wanted – with a route that introduced a browser, presented our Hunters' credentials and then allowed the browser to view on-screen ties, with some basic interaction, then make a purchase.

At this stage in the building process (now some three months after the US Marine Corps experience) our knowledge of how the internet worked was increasing at an incredible rate. It is important to keep up with developments and we were already allocating an hour each day for one of us to be conducting 'live' field research (surfing). Eventually we decided to expand this into the evenings and weekends, increasing our research to 10 hours a day – as our phone bills testified!

It is imperative that your research be continuous, and not just a quick one-off look at other people's sites. You are entering a totally different business world – some techniques that you have been using will apply, but many others will not.

Quality training creates a mindset that is conversant with the technology. Ultimately that training will eclipse your original browser's expectations – it has to as your knowledge limit keeps moving forward and as you think, so you create.

We are firm believers in training (we have been through enough management courses), but there's always something new to learn. It's how you relate that learning to your current situation that will increase your capability to deliver an engaging proposition to your browser audience.

The conclusion we drew from our own research was that the internet channel in our sector was wide open, despite the high number of competitor websites. Even if sales did not materialize, the chances were that we would have a valuable on-line interactive presence to underpin our brand. This itself would increase our standing in the eyes of our retail customers as our website would be a valuable information point to which they could direct customers' questions with regard to our brand and ties.

Site building problems

Once we had designed the site to our growing knowledge level, we were then able to pass the information to Internet Assist.

However, through our own 'we know best attitude' we created a problem for ourselves as we tried to manage the building process of the site in much the same way that we would a normal commercial project. Our plan contained fixed parameters regarding the display output level (what a browser would see) and was only functional up to our technical level and knowledge at the time.

Clearly this was the wrong approach. The first fully operational website was basically what we had asked for but looked different from what we had imagined, and while the concept we had devised worked, the overall look of the site made it uncommercial. In short it was what we were already doing on paper, but now it was on computer. It just didn't represent us as a luxury brand and looked more like something that was made to look old – a bit like reproduction furniture.

Flexibility of the site and its functionality are paramount. There is no point reproducing what you already do, down to the last detail. We realized that we had to consider our LuxuryTies e-venture as a totally new and separate business start-up in the fullest sense of the words. The whole process of development is different as the technology moves fast and markets chase the latest on-line innovations.

We have to think differently about the sales channel represented by LuxuryTies and support this by knowledge acquisition (or learning as it used to be called!). As stated earlier, have a fixed goal but make the route to it flexible – we lost a lot of time by not doing that.

E-businesses are all about flexibility. They must be positioned to respond to changing markets, and must have updating capabilities to keep reinforcing a market leadership position.

As such, we consider that websites themselves have a shelf-life because browsers or consumers will tire and new sites will arrive that eclipse your own if you fail to manage the IT correctly.

Whatever site you deploy, the updating ability must be sufficient to retain the original message while reinventing itself. We achieve this through new designs, optimization, newsletters and multimedia technology upgrades, which for LuxuryTies has included on-line video showing how to tie a Windsor (style of tie knot), a bow tie, etc.

All this should prove that rather than writing an all-singing, all-dancing business plan, it is better to build your site based on customer-focused technical experience. You should concentrate on your business area of specialization as a more open and evolving goal-led activity, which itself is driven by the consumer's use of technology in your market. It is then how you position and deploy the technology to attract customers that determines success or failure.

When dealing with ever changing technology that is sales focused, the end browsers' own technological capability and need for an experience within an on-line environment keeps advancing. Effectively the people who are looking at your website are themselves becoming smarter in their use of technology, and this includes acceptance and understanding of the technology used to engage them and what it can deliver over the phone line.

People get bored of the basics. We all want to witness new experiences, and browser loyalty is a rare commodity – especially in a virtual high street for luxury ties with 580,000 e-stores with the same product and the same opening hours!

Following our understanding that internet users were themselves getting smarter, our market message evolved around the capabilities of LuxuryTies. We identifed new user groups that we had not considered before but which could turn out to be larger than our original consumer group, for example the gift market (such as Father's Day), or those who just enjoy looking at and using new technologies – indeed, we receive many orders from people who own and work in computer companies.

Positioning the site to meet as many of these identified groups as possible would therefore require a wider sphere of promotion. When optimization was employed as a substitute for advertising we would then be able to reach the wider, more diverse markets for our product type, and our company and its brand message would be interpreted differently by the various user groups we chose or selected to optimize the site towards.

Ultimately, we do not want to restrict our market to tie wearers. People who browse LuxuryTies are just as important as people who buy from it. A visit has an almost future bankable element through our collection of browser site registrations (explained in Part 3) when we run newsletter campaigns to promote the change-over in our on-line tie cabinets.

Stage 4 – Delivering a total experience

Once we understood the issues outlined in Figure 3.5 we could start to integrate LuxuryTies into our existing b2b business model. Initial changes we decided on included enlarging the role of our commissioned salesmen in our export markets to become our site representatives, acting as local LuxuryTies points of contact in their native countries. This would give us a bit more browser/buyer confidence and a voice in a native tongue on the end of a phone line in the searcher/browser's own country/time zone.

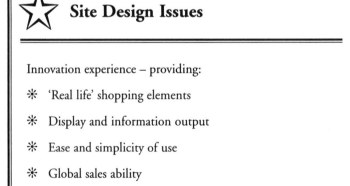

Figure 3.5 Site design issues.

Some organizations are today attempting to establish localized operations but we feel this takes away the fun of the internet. Our customers enjoy dealing with us even though we are, on average, 5,000 miles away. For them it's a case of buying/dealing with the originating source, the fail-safe being that there is someone nearby they can speak to if a problem arises.

To give browsers some incentive to try out your website you must offer a new product or experience-based process that is not available in an off-line environment. The following extract from the American periodical *Tulsa World*, is taken from an article which also included a review of our site entitled 'No Frills Book Provides Key To Problem Solving':

> Speaking of time wasters, I couldn't believe I was actually standing over my scanner the other night, trying to arrange a dress shirt so I could get a good image of the collar and first three or four buttons.
>
> I'd been suckered in by a website called LuxuryTies.com, which (as the name implies) hawks upscale neckwear from Hunters, the British clothing manufacturer. The premise of the site is that you'd be a fool to spend $80 or $100 on a necktie without knowing whether it matches your shirt. So LuxuryTies provides a virtual dressing room where you can click on an image of a tie and then 'drag' it over to the shirt of your choice.
>
> Hunters offers a variety of generic shirt images in different patterns and colors, but you can also scan in an image of your own shirt and use it for a perfect match. Strangely enough, this actually worked when I tried it.
>
> (© 2000 Bell & Howell Learning & Information Services)

This did make us a smile – outside positive accreditation is always good news, even if we did have the term 'hawk' applied to us, to which we can only comment: 'Sir, this is Savile Row. We don't hawk – we present.'

We don't think the internet has replaced conventional shopping, but do feel that one day it will account for a very large share of all sales, especially as novel experiences can be delivered. The 'virtual dressing room' explanation of what we designed had re-named what we had done.

Overall high on-line purchase volumes are still a long way off at present. For now, the internet has to be used to sell in an imaginative way. Otherwise what reason has someone got to visit your website other than just a quick price check before buying from somewhere else?

The message here is that you have to create an on-line experience (just as we did for the reviewer in Tulsa) that goes beyond your primary market and reaches into new markets through a compelling and imaginative use of technology.

Revamping a value chain in any business will create a new culture, as what was once of importance might now become secondary. Prior to our site we had very little contact with the public at large. This was a secondary activity of Hunters as we always dealt with the store buyers first. Now we have to adapt to credit card payments, individual dispatch of items and management of the website itself.

On this last point it is worth noting, as we begin to move towards Part 2, that a website cannot just be launched. The idea that you invent, build and register with the search engines is only part of the process.

For us, rankings within any search engine are 'front and centre'. We want to be a top ten website for our product class in a cyber environment where there are 580,000 tie and related accessories competitor websites operational at any one time – and they keep growing in number!

The value chain development at Hunters must now incorporate website management (entailing site rankings, position analysis, incentives, public relations, etc to keep us in our market's browser) as a primary issue, coupled with continually delivering innovation to our audience to develop the Hunters' brand platform via LuxuryTies.

CHAPTER 4

Case study: conclusions and epilogue

Conclusions

Depending on what you feel a web presence does for your company, be it as an information centre or a new sales function, there will be significant impacts in a variety of areas. For us the main purpose is the establishment of a direct b2c sales revenue stream and brand platform, with ourselves as the controlling influence behind the Hunters' brand credentials.

We anticipate that a web presence can increase our sales by up to 60% over a two-year period in relation to our current direct to retail b2b activity. In doing so this will generate significant savings on our fixed cost overheads – this is what a website should or will be doing for you, provided the market likes what you are about.

As stated, there is no point in trying to run the same business that you currently have, on-line, as it will just lead to duplication of effort. The effective take-up level will not be as high as you would expect as there are no new end-user benefits. Why stay in the same market when you can reinvent yourself in another which may turn out to be more profitable than all your current activities combined?

Some managers will doubt these words, arguing that it is possible to act in just the same manner and employ a website as a back-up function to underpin an existing value-added service/product.

To this we would reply that businesses will not operate in the way they currently do five years from now. The amazing growth in this area has already put too many fund managers at risk as they back 'hot' e-shares with high future growth expectations. Thus performance and change will be demanded in almost all businesses, especially those e-businesses that won investment when the market was buoyant.

We also expect new types of competition to emerge within the next two years, formed of both increased price competitiveness and new channel competition. Traditional methods of displaying and selling goods will be put under pressure by technology. Television has been cited as the next-generation internet delivery method, drawing on computer technology. Indeed, some forward-thinking organizations are already pioneering in this field.

Retailers, for example, are beginning to add large plasma TV screens to their shop windows. At certain times of the day the shop window display changes, enabling the store to reach a particular target shopper group, segmented by age, more effectively. The expense of continually having to physically alter the shop window is thus avoided by timed alterations to the store's own visual messages, managed through computer-generated high-resolution images operated by the store's head office anywhere in the world. At the push of a button all store windows can be restyled to reflect a theme or special offer promotion targeted at a specific age group.

M-commerce (via the mobile phone) is also advancing at great speed. Soon, as a consumer in a store looking at a certain product, you will be able to type into your mobile phone the product description/brand/name/price of what it is you are looking at, and within seconds your phone will give you details of alternative stores within a five block radius that have the same product for less!

Therefore competition between the traditional and the new will increase. All that can be said at the moment is that sales via the internet continue to grow, and each month thousands more organizations and people join in. Great new technologies are being developed that engage people and hold their interest. At the same time product horizons are broadened, with consumers expecting more from everything they buy and own, as the information behind the products and brands becomes more readily available.

Epilogue

Eventually our own expectations of the internet changed. Where once we wanted just to increase sales, eventually we aspired to create the most unique and advanced website for ties in the world. After all, what did we have to lose? As a small unfunded business we were without constraints, with nothing more than a blank piece of paper and an idea.

We realize that the whole web concept is still in an evolutionary stage. You can create and reinvent your company overnight on a limited budget, providing you take the time to understand the whole process involved in delivering a unique browser experience focused towards existing consumer habits.

Half the fun of mastering the internet is that if you can understand how it works your website design will win, because you will produce a site that fits in with the internet principle of enjoyment.

One year after launching LuxuryTies.com, we had achieved thousands of pounds worth of orders, media and press from all over the world – all from watching people arguing about which tie matches which shirt and working out a way of replicating that on-line!

The best media coverage we ever managed to win was a review by the *New York Sunday Times* business section. One of our b2b customers wrote to us afterwards saying 'a full page in the NYT means you've made it' – how many of the funded dotcoms ever got that?

We later learned that marketing and PR executives dream of winning their clients a 'score' in this newspaper. Maybe they could if they stopped and really thought about what is important to the end customer rather than hyping up websites that have failed to live up to expectations.

A while after the NYT article we had a phone call from an executive at one of the world's most famous luxury brands, congratulating us and saying we had caused quite a stir in his marketing department.

We were both very proud. People all over the world had noticed us, giving different names to our on-line creation. That is what brand acceptance is – interpretation into your customers' own thought patterns and lifestyle codes.

This all validates our earlier efforts in trudging round the streets of New York starving hungry and dreaming of creating a meaningful brand. Had we known then what we know now, that one day the NYT would write about us along with all the other media, I think we would have regarded it as just ridiculous, and filed it along with all the other wishful thinking.

What's difficult to explain is the natural affinity we have with the USA. We can't define why people there fell in love with what we did, but they have and we continue to enjoy all the e-mail enquiries and orders we receive, making a point of (on occasion) telephoning customers to introduce ourselves, and always personally signing the thank you letters that accompany our ties when dispatched to their new owners.

Today, we look back at projects like our direct e-mail questionnaire which, although basic, proved that a market exists for Savile Row ties on-line and that people would take the time to fill out forms despite today's pressurized working conditions. All this led to the website we have today.

There is a constant need, now more than ever, for all companies to improve what they are doing and move closer to their final end markets. Internet trading satisfies this need to give assurance of long-term survival and future development.

Ultimately what drove us was the creation of a site that would be unique in our product class, but what influenced us was the way in which we could emulate a real-life shopping experience that was just as enjoyable as real life itself. If you can get all this to work simultaneously in your favour you will have an internet presence that's going to be fantastic! People will want to visit your site for the experience alone and will want to learn about you and, we are sure, will want to buy from you.

But you have to ensure that your site is visible within the search engines (who don't actually index about two-thirds of all websites) and occupies a top rank position for your product or service class. That's the real game: to replace high marketing/advertising expenditure to develop a brand platform. From this case study and its analysis we move on now to introduce you to the concepts of segmented and differentiated brand marketing through site optimization and focused search engine tuning.

PART 2

Developing an on-line brand

CHAPTER 5

Starting to think about optimization

Identifying key issues from your current business model

LuxuryTies was originally designed to increase Hunters' own sales and support an emerging brand. Figure 5.1 overleaf forms the background to this chapter.

Any organization that says it doesn't need to build sales should look back at the many failures that litter the world of business and not just e-commerce. If sales and evolving markets were never an issue we would still be dealing with organizations set up at the dawning of time, and they would be massive by now.

We all know that sales are the critical and driving factor regardless of whether you are on or off-line. However it's the route a business takes to generate sales in a profitable and simple way that can be the deciding factor between success and failure. Overly complex business models themselves are fraught with danger, as often they require too many variables to interact simultaneously. When e-commerce is brought into the frame these variables can be dispersed over vast distances, causing further problems in control.

The internet has proved itself as the global sales tool it was 'billed' as. Today organizations can easily reach those larger markets, reinvent themselves and be all the things the start-up books say they can be, in a simple and fairly efficient

www.LuxuryTies.com

Launched April 2000, achieving:

❊ Brand equity development

❊ Membership database growing

❊ 70,000 unique visitors – 1 million hits – sticky

❊ Repeat on-line orders emerging

❊ External validation – globally – case studies etc

Figure 5.1 LuxuryTies.com: background information.

manner – from even a bedroom or garden shed, as some of the successful start-ups know.

Like us, the vast majority of businesses in the world are small. Indeed most UK companies are small businesses (our definition of a small business is a company with a turnover of less than £500,000) servicing local communities. Today those communities have a wider range of choice, which often goes beyond what their own local small businesses can provide, as a direct result of the new and emerging technologies.

In many cases the customer proposition available on-line is better than what the local off-line small business can deliver, and once again the axe hangs over the head of the small or micro business community. The difference this time is that it's a global axe. At Hunters we compete with similar companies in Greece, Italy and elsewhere around the globe for the same common website browser and necktie wearer.

Thus the question arises: how can a small business use its current model to identify issues within its market(s) and then generate revenues from it? From the Hunters' case study the problems we faced may be summarized as follows:

• a need to go on-line, having found a way to engage a wider market

• limited cash-flow resource to develop out

• conflicting interest – Hunters would compete with its existing retail customer base for the same end customer

- competition was and is intense – the funded businesses could throw money into advertising

- a new brand in a business lacking the skill set to develop an e-commerce application.

Once we had identified the main issues that restricted Hunters' growth we compartmentalized them into standard core business areas.

If you analyze the issues above you will find that they actually relate to:

- finance

- marketing

- technology.

All three are linked together, impacting upon one another, but only one holds the real key to success that will alleviate the significance of the others, shifting the focus of a 'problem' to become a challenge.

The first step we took was to summarize our problem in a single clear and focused paragraph:

> Following the website's design and definition around the market's existing purchasing habits, how – on little or no money – could we market our site to create sales once the site was launched?

We decided that the route to follow would be marketing based on value-added technology innovation. If we continued to ensure that sales were what led the business everything else would fall into place.

As the option we selected required being trained in areas new to us, the decision to go forward was hard to make as we were already trying to do too much, and to start allocating longer training periods was going to be difficult. However, the internet actually enabled our training as we undertook lectures on-line from a Californian school, and followed this with Dean Markham's own programme, learning and working on LuxuryTies at the same time.

Eventually this learning lost its training tag and became a form of business development (or on-the-job-training!). As we began to see and reap the benefits of our efforts over a fairly short time scale (about two months) our enthusiasm and skill set grew continually – the more we learned the more the site earned and the higher up the ranks we went.

However, we were in a Catch 22 situation: we identified very early on that to sell Hunters' ties to the bigger end market we needed to have the website, but for this we had to generate additional cash to develop it, and for the training required to understand the technology involved.

Hunters as a business has many constraints and, due to our constant battle with cash flow, we failed to check our business goals against our market's changing habits. Today we undertake a regular check-up of what we are about and where we are in relation to our goals, adjusting them as necessary and undertaking ad hoc training when the need identifies itself, to make sure we can capitalize on opportunities whenever we identify them.

Like us, you will find that cash is the answer to all your problems – it buys you time. While time and cash are interchangeable, like many small businesses we cannot secure VC funding and therefore we have to organize all the other media that are either free or low in cost to generate customers that convert into sales quickly. Today we continually shop around for 'free offers' from the business community, in the hope that one in a hundred will be worth trying out.

When you have completed your first issue analysis and focused on the problems within your company, you can then start to compartmentalize them into different areas and work round the difficult issues, picking off the easy ones first just as we did.

By the time you have dealt with most of the easy problems the biggest won't look that difficult, and you will be able to simplify the matter through the creation of small sub-solutions. Most of the time a problem is only a problem because you lack knowledge of the area causing difficulties. Once you have that knowledge you have the solution and then it's just a matter of applying your new knowledge in a coherent manner.

The solution to our issue was optimization training and then deployment of our new skills as a substitute for costly advertising. Like all those new to the internet at that time, we were originally convinced by the pundits that the best way to create on-line sales was to advertise like mad as 'this was the only way to generate the large volume of continuous site visitors'.

We nearly believed this rubbish. We wonder how many businesses could have started up if they had realized there was a simple way round the problem but were put off when they discovered the costs of advertising/marketing to engage an audience, especially the average customer acquisition cost of $89.00.

Whoever thinks these statistics up has probably never been in business but takes their data from big funded sites which throw money into advertising products that no one in their right mind wants. Of course its going to be expensive to sell junk, and what that statistic says to us is that it costs an average

$89.00 to con someone into buying something that's really only worth $9.99 thus achieving a loss of some $79.01 per sale. And if you do that enough times, guess what? You go out of business!

Today, the irony is that on-line businesses that have survived without VC money (such as us) are stronger than the businesses that had the funding. And there's a good chance that after reading this text you will be around long after they have spent the last drop of their VC's money trying to find that secret key to sales – which we have always known is giving customers something they want, in the way they want it and figuring out a way to help the market find it.

Really, it's not a difficult concept to understand, but many funded start-ups made it difficult. Old-timer management was brought in from the off-line corporates who could only function in complex structures, the more complex the better as it made them feel like they were doing a worthwhile job. It was fashionable to join a dotcom with a big wealth creation bond (share options they could convert on flotation) on the back of it.

As we read about those 'big name managers' joining these start-ups, we realized that for most this was their last chance to make some quick money to retire on – and many did, leaving the businesses they were involved in to crash and burn, and ultimately leaving the shareholders to pick up the tab.

You might think this is cynical of us but it's the reality. Once we learned how the whole 'game' worked we stepped away from it, deciding we'd make it on our own.

There will be a few out there who dispute these words, saying their involvement was necessary to get the business going, but – and here's the crux of the argument – spending someone else's money is easy, spending your own is harder, especially when the roof over your head is at risk. We can all waste money – there's no skill in that – and these big corporate guys played with someone else's money, and just as importantly someone else's dreams along with the jobs of employees who tried hard, only to be sold out.

We still meet many old-school corporate bosses. These days they phone us selling their 'consultancy skills', trying to enthuse us with the names of the big companies they 'survived' in for 20 years and the dotcoms they wrecked, and palming off their failures with generalizations such as 'consolidation' 'business model convergence', etc. Our game when they call is to try and sell them something – that's poetic justice.

Let's face it, as these corporate guys didn't start the businesses they whiled away their 'careers' in, what possible use could they be to a technology-based start-up? Most of them lived in fear of customers and computers.

Understanding website optimization marketing processes

After being turned down for funding more times than we care to remember, we realized that we were going to exist outside the mainstream website business world.

But we had a few theories and ideas that we had identified during our early research, which would prove useful in the future as we struggled towards our goals. Perhaps the first and most important was that some form of commonality must exist for websites to perform in the way they did (and mostly still do), with or without VC funding.

The primary browser platform upon which all websites rest is, in our opinion, the search engines and directories of which there are about 20 major examples – including the likes of MSN, AOL (both search engines) and directories such as Yahoo!.

If these platforms are the start of the route that people take (the searcher or browser) to find your products/services then these search engines and directories are vitally important. (Eventually we went on to imagine the engines/directories as a form of virtual high street with rows and rows of stores stretching off into the horizon, into which we, as people searching for products/services, are parachuted.)

The LuxuryTies critical marketing issue was then summarized further following these thoughts:

> Just how do we get LuxuryTies to a number one position on the search engines and directories so that when a searcher types in the word 'TIES' our site is the first they see, or at worst is in the first three pages for any other identified generic search term(s) that a browser who wants to buy a tie might be using?

This is the goal of optimization. However, before we can start looking into it in any great detail, it is necessary to list the critical issues that surround your business, beginning with sales and then working down; learning from scratch why your goal is what it is and understanding what you really want to achieve from your on-line business.

You will find that the issues you have detailed are the same as ours, albeit in a different order. And if your objective in reading this text is to increase your website revenues, you should by now have begun to take a different view of the importance of developing innovative brands and high website ranking positions within the search engines and directories.

Having now defined our critical issue, we came to realize that the solution lay in low-cost search engine optimization tactics and to recognize the importance of this medium in the promotion frame. At that time many organizations paid no attention (and many still don't) to the importance of the first step in the consumer's purchase route, ie the search engines or directories. It is these search engines or directories that control what people see in terms of the websites returned following a search. You may have a great website, but if no one can find it, what's the point?

Targeting the search engines and directories

Note: Today technological innovation itself has a shelf-life, and it can be emulated and copied almost instantaneously. It is not the ultimate source of competitive advantage but it can form the foundation from which you emerge as the market leader. Thereafter it is your job to discover a tactic that retains your dominant position and maintain this.

All countries have searchable databases of one type or another. Some are specific to their locality – in the US, for example, many are localized towards small towns servicing their own communities. Our own research found about 17,500 minor engines and directories scattered around the internet, although this number is on the increase as more specialized engines and directories emerge to meet a growing browser base, whose requirements in terms of relevancy of results continues to increase.

On discovering this, we realized that attempting to be on each and every searchable database was going to be a massive job in its own right. While this is conceivable, checking through the reams of positioning information and making continual adjustments to achieve high rankings would be next to physically impossible, unless you could afford the high cost of outsourcing this function. So, the first step we took was to review as many of the directories and engines as we could and eventually decided to focus our energies and activities on the major 20 globally renowned ones, as these account for the majority of web traffic.

What we learnt as we studied each one was (and not unsurprisingly you might think) that they are all different. Many have the same websites indexed but that's about the only similarity we could find on our first review.

However, as we looked closer we began to find massive differences between them which make them all unique. They each operate the search response differently and have, in effect, a specific type of programming language to interpret your website's own programming language, including the style of your home page's word placement/text alignment. This can have either a good or bad effect on your eventual website rankings/target market.

With our knowledge of entering and developing export markets we were able to interpret this experience as if the search engines and databases were themselves individual foreign countries. We identified the characteristics that made each unique, enabling us to create an ongoing search engine/database marketing programme for LuxuryTies that was based on the engines and directories in which we were most interested.

Once we started to think about the searchable databases in this way we were able to study each one to discover what was key, in terms of the type of results returned, when we searched under alternative generic product words and phrases relevant to our website. We were also able to review the main brands presented within the search results with a view to understanding why these websites were in the top ten for words and terms specific to our product sector, eg ties, neckties, etc.

We then started to realize (just as we did in our off-line markets) that being seen alongside the major brands (which were often in the top search engine positions) would be enough for our browser community to regard LuxuryTies as 'just as good as them'. The focus of our challenge intensified to become: how do we get there and are there any spin-off benefits that we can capitalize on?

Collecting browser/searcher data from the search engines and directories

These main searchable databases have built up valuable demographic information regarding the type of browser who most commonly uses them, to . the point where some have defined the median age range, income and lifestyles of their users.

This research is valid. When we undertook our own research into which engine and directories our friends were using, a pattern emerged that actually did fit (albeit broadly) the demographic data being presented by the engines in their marketing information and in some cases their share prospectus – the public information that was available under the 'investor' section of their site.

Our plan was to rank in order which of the searchable engines and databases would be targeting, through their own advertising and marketing operation, the consumer groups profiled by LuxuryTies or had a growing browser/visitor base that fitted with our profiled purchaser and concentrate our optimization towards them. This would actually save us the cost of advertising to a specific browser group, as the primary target market (the search engine/database) is working for us in isolating our buyer or browser grouping in a bid to retain and increase their own users of a certain demographic type.

For example, if you make a trendy product aimed at the twenty-year-old age group you first have to take into consideration those search engines/databases that visitors or potential customers of your profiled kind are most likely to visit to perform their searches. You then channel your efforts into creating an engaging and compelling site/message programming tactic that meets this target market first through the selected search engine. In optimizing towards a target market in this way you are adopting a concentration strategy that is safer and cheaper than attempting a 'land grab'.

Knowing that each of the searchable databases has a different core market of loyal browsers/users means that you can fine-tune your efforts towards those databases whose browser grouping would buy into your brand message as pertinent to its lifestyle or needs. Another way to think about this concept is: would you advertise a vintage Rolls Royce in a used auto magazine or with a classic car auctioneer?

Look and learn where your browser type visits. Review the search engines and directories regularly to ensure their style meets your own target market's needs.

Generating focused traffic from the main search engines/directories

As our research continued, we found a recurring slogan being used by the website optimizing consultants and the search engines/directories themselves:

85% of all website traffic comes from the main search engines/directories.

This is one statistic we believe. Coming across it in enough credible sources confirmed to us that the traditional advertising and marketing operations that an organization like Hunters could get involved in were next to useless in an e-commerce environment. This has been proven by the high failure level among the pure dotcom businesses with their land-grabbing approach to winning new markets, including TV ads, hard copy media, spam e-mails and so on.

One of the main problems we encountered was that so many new e-businesses were advertised in one go that no sooner had you read or seen one ad than you were on to the next, having forgotten completely about the last!

During a series of presentations in the summer of 2000 we stated that the only people making money out of e-commerce were the guys at the ad companies. The reasons for this are simple:

- Most of those old-timer CEOs were so used to having marketing departments under their control that they brought into the new dotcom companies their old cronies to manage this function (a.k.a. jobs for the boys).

- These cronies then employed the same organizations that were advertising their ex-employers' businesses because they were familiar with them and had some previous relationship. They accepted without question the presentations (and invoices) of the advertising companies who thought they had devised really awesome campaigns to support the new products/services and new delivery mechanisms – but which were total rubbish!

We have no gripe with the advertising companies. In fact we wish we had been in that field at the time as it was money for old rope.

That aside, Figures 5.2 and 5.3 below show, in a very basic manner, how a website that has been optimized for the generic terms specific to our product class of the keywords 'ties, neckties and neckwear' has more chance of being found by browsers who are searching for websites selling ties under these alternative search words/phrases.

By understanding that the search engines and directories are the common interface between a browser and website you will realize that the main aim of optimization is to make sure you are returned in the top results, and not just by one but by as many as possible of your selected engines and directories, for variations of your product/service generic terms or phrases that a browser would normally use.

Many organizations tend to opt for words/phrases that are industry jargon – too obscure for the normal outsider to know or to apply to the product/service for which they are searching. IT people must take the blame for this as they often fail to explain in full the importance of optimization when developing websites.

One of the best ways to find those keywords that browsers or searchers most commonly use when they are looking for the type of offering you have, is to ask people outside your organization what words they would use to describe what you have for sale. In this way we created a list, ranking the most frequently recurring term first, the next second and so on. Later in this book we will show you how to deploy this information.

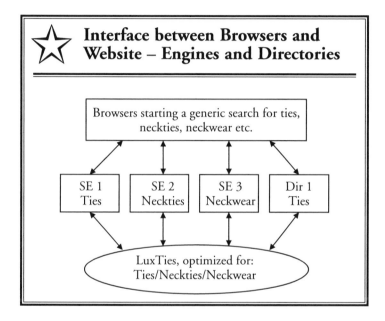

Figure 5.2 Engines and directories as the interface between browser and website.

As you can see from Figure 5.2 we portray the traffic flowing between searcher, engine/directory and website. The more browsers that see your brand name the better when it is linked to a generic product type search or a search for specific phrases.

But what happens to a website's traffic when the site hasn't been optimized towards any specific words or phrases? This is depicted in Figure 5.3 overleaf.

In this instance, as the website is not correctly or fully optimized the searcher will not find you but will end up on other optimized websites. Meanwhile, you will be left wondering why the website and e-business you designed and planned gets no visitors and therefore makes no sales.

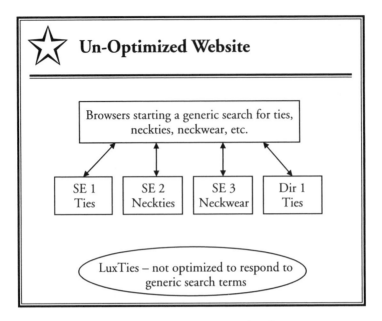

Figure 5.3 An un-optimized website.

This continues to be a common fault among websites, and it's by ignoring the importance of the search engines and directories as the primary information markets that websites remain unknown.

Using the search engines in your marketing

We learned early on that you cannot apply a single thematic message to your markets and approach them in a scattergun fashion, in the hope that one market will emerge as the leader and will cover the cost of the advertising expense wasted on other markets where there has been little or no take up. But many of the funded dotcoms tried to prove that just such a land-grab approach could work!

While they were all busy testing that theory out with their VC's money, we found that you can optimize independently to each of the search engines and directories (the primary market) while retaining your basic brand credentials. This is achieved by focusing more on certain words/terms in some engines than on others, depending on the browser using the engine.

We were then able to adapt the term/phrase to the search engine/directory user base following a review of the browser demographics. As some engines attract more mature surfers than others, it therefore makes sense to employ words, terms and phrases that a browser in a senior age bracket would use when they conduct a search for products in our class using a certain engine specific to their needs.

For example, SE1 (see Figures 5.2/3) draws in a professional young audience searching mainly under the phrase 'designer brand ties', whereas SE3 attracts a more mature age range for whom the most frequently used generic product search term for ties is 'neckwear'. It's the same product at the end of the line but a different search language is used by browsers depending on the engines/directories they are on. This is a result of each engine's own marketing positioning and pull message, which creates their browser/user base.

The steps we took were to find out which engines attracted the customer profile that we had established was responsive to our brand, through the demographic data published on their visitors. We then optimized towards their browsers in their own search language having found the highest ranking search terms applicable to our product class in the engines.

It should be noted that just like a traditional project to enter a new market, success depends on how well can you research that target market – in this case how well you can adapt your original message to engage target browsers in different cultures and using different search terms.

Figure 5.4 overleaf is a table showing the number of websites within two engines that are optimized to respond to generic searches for a series of tie-related words/phrases. LuxuryTies' position is also shown in relation to these websites for similar products during the summer of 2001. (This should give you an idea of how competitive our sector is.) Mostly the websites indexed by both search engines are the same (ie what we found on AltaVista we also found on Lycos), although Lycos is three times larger than AltaVista for our product class in terms of the number of websites indexed by them selling ties.

During May 2000 we were fortunate to be invited to appear on a satellite TV business programme, and it was there that we were asked what was the 'secret of our success'! We believe it was our early identification of the importance of the demographic profiling of the visitors to the search engines/databases we had selected, where optimization could underpin a promotional programme for brand development on a near zero budget, providing the site responded to the target audience's language.

Once we had 'trained' LuxuryTies to achieve that, we could employ focused brand message tactics, based on the fact that we knew the 'language' our

Figure 5.4

Generic term	No of sites on:		GoTo search term analysis*	LuxuryTies highest ranking position**
	AltaVista	Lycos		
Ties	542,626	1,616,579	15,134	6
Neck ties***	23,864	25,872	9,279	5
Neckwear	24,101	52,024	517	–
Men's ties	164	383	1,376	–
Savile Row	845,274	6,192	555	1
Matching shirts and ties	4,686,309	5,950	104	1

* GoTo operate a service that tells you the number of times a word or phrase has been used the month previously in a web query or search. At the time of writing, that service can be accessed from the *www.payperclicktools.com* website.

** The highest position LuxuryTies.com has achieved under these search terms across any of the main engines.

*** The terms 'neckties' and 'neck ties' produced the same results for both engines, indicating that the space separating the words is irrelevant in a browser's search and would not alter the rankings or the results returned to the browser.

audience would use to search for our type of product within, and specific to, the search engines/directories we were targeting.

If you know where your market exists (or visits most often), coupled with the language it speaks (ie the phrases/terms it uses to find products like yours), the main issue of identifying a market becomes far simpler. However, most businesses spend years and significant sums of money trying to locate the optimum low-cost route to market, when in fact, the search engines and directories will do all that for you for nothing.

During the same TV interview referred to above, it was put to us that out of the 14 million websites operational at that time only 30,000 were making any money! This is difficult to comment on. However, the main reasons for this would seem to be: trying to repackage and sell other organizations' brands; a lack of optimization; and an inability to create/deliver an experience-based, value-added product enhancement on-line that would be of direct benefit or enjoyment to the browser.

We will return to techniques of optimization in more detail later in this book. At this point, however, it will remain in the background as we describe further the creation of LuxuryTies and how it was launched and marketed to evolve as a site that gives a user a particular experience, and where we regarded the marketing use/role of optimization as crucial to achieve our business development goal.

CHAPTER 6

Being an on-line brand

It takes just as much time to develop a loser as it does a winner!
(Booze, Allen & Hamilton, 1968)

We are always surprised by the number of people who regard the development of a brand as just the creation of a logo. To us the logo is part of the corporate image process (although we have met many in the field of graphical design who can tell us why and with what type of logo a certain product should be represented).

We just can't see how all the swirling words and high-impact colours of a logo can automatically make a customer think of the brand factors than can only be derived through tangible experience based on ownership or on satisfying aspirational needs.

Furthermore, most of the great logos that we know today have evolved over time and are backed up with a product or service suite that has created a loyal following. Bearing that in mind, how can a newly designed logo say and achieve as much when no one has any experience of the product or service being promoted?

Today, if someone says to us that a brand has got to be represented by a logo we immediately think of the costs involved in marketing that logo alone, especially on-line. Again the land-grab theorists fail to understand that a promotion has to go on forever to keep the logo in the eyes of the browser, and in trying to achieve this the company has to have an infinite sum of money available to promote that logo continually the world over.

We agree that the logo has its place in the branding exercise but, to us, it acts as an identifier or a hallmark of a known supplier's product. For example, we can tell you what company X makes just by seeing their logo because it is well supported (marketed, advertised, etc), and as it has been around for a long time the chances are we have had some direct or indirect experience of the product/service it represents.

Therefore we are certain of a couple of facts when we talk about products, brands and their logos:

- The products and services were created long before the logo was ever considered.

- It was the customers who, after experiencing the product or service, then identified with the organization's logo. It is not the other way round, ie the customers saw the new logo and bought the product on the strength that the logo looked nice.

Many, if not all, of the most famous brands are represented by a logo or marque of some kind. But the logo is just one part of the entire branding process and we have to look at its relevancy at the early stage of the brand creation project, where the largest time/cost factors have to be addressed – on and off-line. These may be summarized as:

- creation

- credential establishment

- business/technology model

- media pull

- consumer message.

Any product or service to which a brand marque is applied has to be consistent in its physical make-up. Consider some of the well-known luxury cars on the market today: they have a consistency of excellence in their styling and engineering so that wherever you are in the world you can recognize them just by their shape and – if you need more help – by the logo!

Another great brand example is the fast-food chain McDonald's. Their food tastes the same wherever you go in the world, although it is sometimes localized slightly to meet different needs, and just by the taste most people can tell the difference between McDonald's and Burger King. Both brands have a consistency in their food, its taste and the brand features that goes beyond just the logo.

These are just two off-line examples to illustrate how brands can deliver what they stand for beyond a logo. We now move our thoughts to an on-line environment. What happens in a search where the browser or surfer has a long way to go before they actually see your logo? Or what if they can't see your organization's name amid all the others selling the same product and giving out the same message? What good is just a logo then, and how can we get people to try out our site and learn what we do?

Today, in attempting to establish a brand, many new organizations opt for banner advertising to keep sending the message over. However, we question the ability of banner ad campaigns to develop a brand message let alone deliver the high visitor traffic. Who is going to buy from you if you are, like 99% of the internet population, unknown?

A form of on-line banner blindness has now evolved, where people just don't click on them. How many of us these days tend not even to notice them? This is compounded by the near-saturation advertising campaigns that also fail to create a brand as they are too impersonal, and even e-mail campaigns are becoming regarded as spam (ie junk e-mail). We know at Hunters that it is experience, knowledge and trust that create the great brands.

An on-line advertising bombardment does not create a brand – all it might do is communicate the existence of a product/service but that's about it. Many brands reflect the personalities or lifestyles of the originators (like the creators of the famous fashion houses) and that's the challenge for us as brand marketers – how do we convey a personality and lock into the aspirational needs of purchasers on-line?

Having gained an understanding of what a brand is all about we had to find out what factors we could adapt to create on-line a customer-based relationship that would form and deliver the foundation of the Hunters' brand personality through LuxuryTies. The task is summarized in Figure 6.1 overleaf.

Initially we decided that www.LuxuryTies.com would be the delivery mechanism for the Hunters' brand, through the use of interactive technology to generate browser/site visitor interest. However, the true personality of

Key Brand Influencers

❋ Localized target media

❋ Interactive on-line presence

❋ Knowledge depth – show you are the category leader

❋ Be visible – get involved with your market

❋ Update regularly – personally styled newsletters

❋ Watch the competition!

Figure 6.1 Key influences on branding.

Hunters itself would be Savile Row, with Hunters acting in its normal brand role as an experienced Savile Row Master Silk Tie Maker – the true identity of the Hunters' brand but delivered through the on-line medium of LuxuryTies.

Selling other people's brands vs. developing your own

During our early on-line research we realized that the vast majority of websites were actually either repackaging or selling other organizations' branded products, and were promoting the fact that they were selling brand X merely to give themselves credibility.

If anything, these websites were no more than an extra distribution channel for other well-known brand organizations whose products were now available on-line through that third-party website unrelated to the original source. We watched as these third-party websites poured millions into advertising themselves as credible brands and brand suppliers, in the vain hope that they would evolve as brands themselves on the basis that they gave some value-added benefit to the visitor or browser.

However, one of the main problems with this practice is that just as one website shows a range of, say, shoelaces by a well-known shoelace maker, so too do other websites show the same shoelaces by the same maker but at alternative prices – and in some instances these prices can vary widely.

If there is one lesson we learnt from our own Hunters' brand development programme, it is that of uniqueness. Just as brands themselves are unique, there needs to be careful promotion and protection of that inherent uniqueness coupled with the maintenance of a consistency in terms of the product/service, the display methods and the environment. This includes who the brand is seen alongside, what price is charged for it and the support messages used in its promotion.

As soon as a brand becomes traded through on price (a consistency factor) it loses its 'feel' of exclusivity – that's all mass marketing ever does. Once everyone owns it that's the brand's status gone, leaving those consumers who bought it at a higher price feeling cheated – and that's the brand's trust factor lost.

If you take a moment to reflect on some of the once famous brands that have existed, and then think why they no longer occupy a special place in our minds, you'll realize that it was due to the fact that they suddenly become available to everyone – normally at less than their original price – thus losing their value in ownership to us as consumers.

However, a lot of the earlier websites felt that in repackaging another organization's branded products they would be able to defeat the stores (or any other traditional channel) on factors of price and delivery alone – another expensive lesson for the venture capitalists!

Also those earlier (and a number of current) websites decided in their repackaging of brands that increased product content (ie written information) was the 'key' feature in making a sale. The editorial commentary on some websites simply verged on insanity. In one instance we found ourselves in a meeting, being told the benefits of writing pages of 'compelling editorial' sales information to support a wallet alongside its picture. Our thoughts after the meeting were: how on earth could someone write pages on the ownership benefits of a leather wallet? If you are selling a visual product, *just increase the visuals*. Don't try and alter the original brand message with estate agent style copy!

This particular website also wanted to run a range of Hunters' ties. We turned them down as we didn't think they knew what a customer looked like, let alone how to address one. Interestingly enough at the time of writing we did a search to see how they were getting along, only to be presented with a page telling us that the address is no longer available!

Most of these site content managers actually believed they could rewrite why the brands were so unique. They failed to take into account that a brand means different things to different people, as they possess hidden messages that are only activated at certain times of our lives. People as consumers all have subconscious codes and have formed their own 'opinion' of the brand's personality and how the brand meets their particular needs. The logo identifies the product to the consumer when the consumer is faced with a number of similar products – in this instance the logo becomes the identifier between one supplier and another.

The messages put over by the logo are translated by the consumer when viewing products or services from which they derive personal benefit through ownership, and these messages cannot be replaced purely by the written word as a substitute for the experience which, on-line, a consumer is only able to envisage.

At Hunters we know that a brand should never be taken out of its 'natural environment' and should not be promoted by anyone else through their own writings. If you sell a sports trainer shoe make sure it's seen at a sporting event and worn by a sportsperson. Hunters' primary environment is shirts; ties are introduced afterwards because the shirt gets put on before the tie, and therefore on-line we sell a shirt and tie matching service first.

You have to look continually and see how your market already acts with your products/services. You should not try to reinvent the way their life works or the way they would use your product or even a product that is similar.

However, a lot of these new website shopping portals display their brand range products out of their natural environments. Many famous brand products are shown against a stark backdrop of internet white, which looses all the brand's uniqueness and style. When a website does this they just make the brand products appear bland. No imagination or thought could be engendered by the brand at the site visitor/browser level. Which looks better – a smart sports car tearing round the streets of Monte Carlo or that same sports car shown against a plain white canvass? One conjures imaginative thought, the other is just a picture of a car!

Adding value via on-line brand development

We found that the best performing brands on-line need the same tender care and attention as their old off-line counterparts. They should be unique and only available from one (or a limited number) of carefully selected similar channels and must be consistent in all aspects.

The exception is when a known brand product derives value from a third-party website as the association between the two delivers substantial value-added benefit to the brand in some way that creates an additional physical benefit for the end consumer. Through this association a new market may be delivered, or further messages as to the product's superiority may be generated.

Basically, if the website selling the famous brand product could add value to the original brand just by and through this partnership then there is a chance that it could work profitably. If not … forget it! If additional value cannot be added to an existing brand/product by an unknown website there is no point in promoting the displaying website to the market as a brand itself. Moreover, there would be no point in a consumer visiting the website when they could carry out comparative shopping or visit a store for the same or a better value-added proposition/experience.

We realized very early on in our research that this 'added value' could be created and delivered by technology – although one rather well-known dotcom start-up did try this and to its cost learned that the market 'wasn't yet ready for it'. However, perhaps it would have been if the products being offered were unique items that derived enhanced value from the technology presentation/application methods being employed by the dotcom.

LuxuryTies is and was a 'first mover', not for ties but for its use of technology to present and display ties within an interactive brand-conducive Savile Row environment.

LuxuryTies was what it said it was: a high-class men's clothing website, and as Savile Row has an existing reputation for quality men's clothing, the Hunters' brand's own credentials and messages could be set very easily via LuxuryTies.

However, a number of other websites have found that they can add value in their own right to another organization's branded products and have themselves evolved as brands in meeting a new consumer lifestyle or niche segment of the market which the emerging technology has created.

These websites (and there are a number of others we could have selected) are:

- *MP3* – providers of digitalized music to satisfy the demands of youth culture.

- *Amazon* – resellers of thousands of books and CDs at low prices to meet the market of cost-conscious shoppers with diverse interests. Although a third-party brand reseller, Amazon is different as its competitive edge is derived through a wide choice. At Hunters we have great admiration for Amazon's customer care policy – a good brand trust feature.

- *Yahoo!* – a searchable directory providing a high level of relevant results to browser enquiry searches.

All three have a number of common factors:

- They were among the first in their markets – leading the way in their value-added proposition and what the market should expect in terms of choice, styling and the technology required of future market entrants.

- They will, or have, become generic terms for their market – as Hoover is to carpet cleaning so MP3 is to digitalized music for the young.

- They all have (at the time of writing) the financial power to defend and increase their markets. They are big players, and are now established with revenue streams that support them – they will be around for a long time.

- They provide a noticeable value-added difference to existing brand products for the consumer buying from or using these sites. They add value to the original product through ease of access, the provision of new technologies that enhance lifestyles (MP3), data output/search relevancy, competitive prices, a wide selection of products and ease of shopping.

- They are consistent in their quality and environment and have built strong reputations for innovation, value and trust.

As stated, all three organizations were early leaders in their markets. They now control such strong brand platforms that competitors will find it difficult (but not impossible) to emulate. New competitors will emerge to pick off the new segment markets being created by these established websites. The consumer types within these smaller segments will generally want a more specialized/personalized product or service, and as the technology evolves, more can be achieved and can be expected.

The constraints here are that all three organizations – like Hunters with its LuxuryTies website – have to update and upgrade their technological capabilities continually, and search out new and unique products to retain their primary brand leadership positions. This itself can be a daunting prospect if they are to maintain and increase site visitors and 'visitor to sales' conversion rates.

Generic term searches to establish a brand platform

Small on-line companies that are new to the whole branding concept do have a problem. Many cannot be first in the market unless they have a new invention or innovation which is better than anyone else's.

Hunters makes and sells ties, which as a product dates back to the third century BC, and many SMEs like Hunters are single-product organizations, basing their entire business strategies on one core offering.

As single-product companies carry the highest level of risk we believed that achieving some form of brand position would lower this risk. Therefore we decided that we would have to create a linkage from our company name, Hunters, to its generic product type name: ties, on the basis that the more people who know what we do and where our products are available the more sales we can generate.

Really what we want is that when people think of ties the name Hunters springs to mind. We have little or no chance of that ever happening off-line without massive advertising expenditure to communicate our presence, but we can take MP3 as an on-line example – its name does equal music. We tested recall abilities on all three example organizations and each achieved high product to brand name recall in our small research sample.

At Hunters we realize that we can get to the stage where (like MP3) we can use the search engines/directories to give us some of this recall capability and then calibrate a brand message once a search engine has carried out its function. (Imagine that a search engine is like a person with an amazing memory who knows every product and service from every supplier.)

For example, if you type into a browser box 'ties' you get the name LuxuryTies appearing, and if people all over the world who are looking to buy ties get returned to the LuxuryTies website and look at Hunters' ties through the use of our innovative technology, the chances are we will also achieve the generic result for our product class as we have delivered a new experience that is only available with our ties on our website.

We learnt that the quickest way to emulate a generic recall within the search engines was to optimize for generic words, terms and phrases specific to our product type. You should note at this point that advertising only tells people you exist. Optimizing enables people to find you, which is better as these people are actually looking for what you sell or offer, and have a need or interest to buy. Why else would they be searching?

If we focus LuxuryTies on becoming a generic term leader (a generic term is a word or phrase that is used to describe a product universally to its market) within the search engine category for men's ties we have the opportunity to develop a brand through optimization.

At Hunters we felt that if we were ranked within the set of top ten results returned following a generic search under the word 'ties', the chances that Hunters would become well known for ties via LuxuryTies would be greatly increased.

Research showed us that more people search under generic words/phrases to describe a product/sector (ties, flights, music, books, cars, etc) than they do by company/brand name. We also know this through our on-line research. While the highest generic search term is 'sex' (no surprises there!), among the top terms are also the new emerging generic phrases 'MP3' along with 'Yahoo!' and 'Amazon', an impressive result demonstrating that people know what they do and who they are. On-line they have become (or are becoming) the generic terms for their sector's products and services.

As the sites listed as examples are aware, their names have been presented to a browser/searcher following a request for organizations selling their types of products. This means it is free promotion for those organizations when their name is seen at the top of the results, and as they are top of the search engine results their websites are regarded as credible suppliers of music, books, etc.

In our case we realized that if Hunters is the tie brand, LuxuryTies.com becomes the innovative technology medium optimized to respond to the generic keyword 'tie' search induced by browsers, which places LuxuryTies in the top ranking position for the total 'tie' category. As it is returned higher than any other website for this term coupled with it being seen among or above the famous men's clothing brands, LuxuryTies must be regarded as a credible search result and worth a browser's time to look at.

A simpler way to visualize this concept is to imagine all the search engines and directories merged together as one big store with you (a customer) asking at the information desk for a certain product. You are given the results to your request in the order the store has ranked them, and as you trust the information desk in that store, so you trust the results from the search engines/directories.

Moving this example back to the on-line world, it is possible that your website could be in the first top ten results due to optimization without on/off-line advertising and marketing expenditure – as this means nothing to a search engine or directory's website indexing protocols.

When LuxuryTies gets returned in the top results set for a generic search term/phrase enough times within the search engines/directories, then we have a strong foundation for a brand and brand recall proposition (where people can put a product to a company name, ie 'Ties equals Hunters'). This is valuable as organizations spend millions developing and fine-tuning their advertising message to a point where people might see their name alone and think of the product and vice versa.

Most organizations' names today (and their logos!) fail to give any insight into what they do or their product class unless we as consumers are told. Imagine flicking through a phone book and trying to guess what the organizations listed in it do and you have some idea of what optimization can achieve for your website.

Another way to consider the value to you, as a website manager, of the optimization process is to imagine walking into an arena of 100,000 car sales people and announcing you want to buy a car. After the stampede is over, would you talk to everyone or just deal with the ten who responded to you first – as they are the fastest and so have the edge over the other 99,990 sales people?

To illustrate the value of a high generic term search engine recall position, a US company offered us an optimization service for $12,000 per year, and yet they could not guarantee us a top ten slot for the generic keyword 'ties'. Ultimately we managed to achieve it on our own through working with Dean Markham and applying his technical concepts and skills.

Some organizations opt for keyword-rich domain names (where the domain name itself is made up of product generics, bank.com for example) but optimization as a process is valid as most of the top generic phrases were registered at lightning speed many years ago, creating the domain name resale market.

This leaves us all trying to find ways around the problem of low ranking. We overcame the problem through optimization, the premise being that as more domain name extensions are being added (dotTV etc) the more competitive the whole ranking process becomes.

One way we have found to fend off new entrants is to ensure that we beat the generic domain names through a constant optimization process and search engine marketing programme. This delivers LuxuryTies as a top ten browser/searcher visit for our product class through engagement with the technology application and the brand experience that we can deliver.

To us at Hunters the website LuxuryTies is just the store name. We could have called it anything else and still optimized for the tie sector. The aim of optimization is to ensure that the store LuxuryTies responds to the generic tie phrases/term searches and delivers the brand Hunters in the right environment to a browser who is specifically looking to buy ties.

As the search engine lists the organizations in ascending order (and many directories list in alphabetical order) it is fair to think that consumers will regard the website in the number one position as the best, even though it may not be. However, being top of the list is always a big inducement for browsers to visit your site and list position is a good benchmark for assessing websites offering the same product.

Since search engines and directories have become credible suppliers of information, we as consumers naturally believe them when they say this or that website is top of their list for a particular product. We assume the engines are always right and the number one slot is the best company to provide what we are looking for. But what do we think of the websites at the bottom of the list?

Controlling the Hunters' brand credentials via LuxuryTies.com

You're not a specialist if you act like a generalist – to be a specialist, you have to be unique.

During Hunters on-line brand performance evaluation tests, it was decided that the main company product/brand name would remain Hunters as it is unique and sounds very English. Hunters.com was already registered as a website address (URL) when we started our on-line research and therefore, on the advice of Internet Assist, we chose LuxuryTies as the site name. Thus it became a marriage between old and new.

Really, though, as we have said, it doesn't matter too much that the URL name Hunters.com had already been registered by someone else. We realized that we could optimize to ensure we were returned in the results series relevant to our product class regardless of the domain name we gave to the website. However, we knew the name LuxuryTies.com doesn't 'speak' to our market in the same way as our name 'Hunters of London W1' does – it's a matter of tradition and retaining the brand's originating credentials.

Today, we see many organizations dropping the dotcom and any new media extension from their business/company name as this has now become associated with the share collapses and fallout of the new economy. Thus it paid us to continue concentrating on Hunters as the primary brand name.

The website LuxuryTies acts as the display mechanism to present a range of Hunters' design brand ties that are only available on LuxuryTies.com. Once the browser has clicked on the LuxuryTies.com site description (and in many of the first-round search engine submissions our description tag was 'To Tie or Knot To Silk Tie A Necktie' – plenty of generic keywords used!) there is hardly any further reference to the name LuxuryTies in our website – it's all Hunters from there on for the site visitor.

Through optimizing LuxuryTies to respond to generic term searches for ties we do not come under pressure to establish a new brand name in LuxuryTies by traditional advertising and promotional methods. In any event these are expensive and mostly fail to attract the consumer.

Really the choices for us as an organization at the time of launch were:

- Do we stop promoting the Hunters' brand and start promoting LuxuryTies as our brand? *or*

- Do we tell the market that Hunters' ties are available from LuxuryTies.com with the consumer message being encased in a technologically advanced website (LuxuryTies' own added value) to which, when optimized for generic term searches, LuxuryTies would respond?

We realized that if we took the latter route we could employ the process of optimization as the sole marketing tactic to gain a leadership position for our website for the specific generic search terms a browser might use who wanted to buy ties. We could simultaneously introduce such browsers to the Hunters' tie brand to which many people would be new too.

We had to ensure that the Hunters' brand credentials and its Savile Row origins were employed throughout LuxuryTies. This is why the site was designed to look and feel just as someone would expect a traditional London specialist store to be (but on-line) – an image of old England and all that it represents, with its visual messages (ie the picture of the Savile Row street sign) and text wording and placement throughout.

It became very important that our whole site mirrored who we were off-line. If someone had an image of what Savile Row was then we would meet that image. It should be noted that we have people visiting our London showrooms, and therefore the total on and off-line concept has to match or achieve a level of consistency. Indeed, through our earlier b2b business and direct e-mail sales we had gained a great insight into what Savile Row represents to people around the world.

To put this another way, in selling our traditional range of Hunters' ties the website LuxuryTies has to give off the same traditional feel. It could not be a site where there were special offer discounts all over the screen and bright, near-blinding colours – people would not expect that of a Savile Row bespoke tie-maker on or off-line.

Effectively our tactic of LuxuryTies.com hosting Hunters' brand neckties had worked, as more and more people accepted the name Hunters for ties as the originating source. The big difference between us and the 'websites for other people's brands' was that we controlled the Hunters' brand and the complete environment where it could be found, including the pricing and presentation methods – more aspects of brand consistency.

Thus with our site acting as an on-line interactive sales channel, adding value to the main Hunters' brand through technology-never-before-encountered, we made sure it became the only place you could buy a special range of Hunters' design ties on-line.

We are unlike many other shopping websites/portals, which lack any control over the products/brands they are offering. This has led to mass availability, numerous pricing points and emerging issues of consumer confidence. 'You'll find that cheaper if you keeping searching' is a statement frequently heard among e-shoppers, especially with the help of today's comparative shopping websites and devices.

Many of the third-party websites featuring other organizations' brands and products are now under significant pressure to search out new and unique marketable brands. Without them they will ultimately fail to attract visitors thus forcing their closure.

Identifying features of an on-line brand experience

When a browser or searcher visits LuxuryTies the ties themselves are secondary to the experience of mixing and matching shirts to ties – but remember, people are mixing and matching Hunters' ties and even scanning in their own shirts and putting Hunters' ties on them.

Effectively they are receiving a brand experience from using Hunters' ties in this way, but without physical ownership. They have accepted the brand because of that experience, in conjunction with the fact that LuxuryTies has been selected from among the top results returned by a generic search for ties.

As more people looked at the technology in LuxuryTies we realized this was the lever to their purchasing. The route was to check the technology out first, and, finding that it worked, some of the site visitors' subconscious codes had been broken as we were giving enjoyment and offering a new experience.

Thereafter the interaction with ties and shirts became an interesting game, with the end result being the discovery of which tie matched best with any of our on-screen shirts. Once that was decided in the minds of the browsers they generally went ahead and bought the tie they had been moving from shirt to shirt (or interacting with). This pattern was endorsed further as we started to get feedback suggesting that people were buying Hunters' ties as a novelty – they had bought them from 'LuxuryTies', *the* innovative Savile Row website.

During the early stages of website testing, when we sat people down and showed them how the site functioned, we gained some very important feedback – laughter. People who used the site laughed. For us this was a considerable achievement as it meant we would bring enjoyment to tie-wearers: giving the browser an enjoyable experience was a clever concept and would ensure that the LuxuryTies experience would be remembered when looking at competitors' websites.

We began to find that the tie a browser had selected was the kind they would purchase in a store from a competitor brand(s), and, just as if they were in a store, they were able almost to hold the tie in their hand (or mouse). As such, they already owned it as they were interacting with it and starting to think about the ownership benefits of the tie looking good against, say, their existing blue striped shirt.

It was and is the uniqueness and enjoyment of the functionality of choice LuxuryTies provided on-line that ultimately underpinned the uniqueness of the Hunters' brand. Site visitors are within three clicks of gaining this technology experience from the home page to the tie cabinets, and therefore the experience can be derived quickly – an important element of the on-line website visitor's patience to timeframe factor.

Again it is important to restate that the technology itself is just a part of the overall Hunters' brand experience. The ties themselves bear out that experience as we have a high level of repeat purchasers, another feature of a brand.

You may recall from earlier sections of this book that we have over 580,000 competitors on-line selling men's ties and related accessory items. The only possible way they could effectively be taken on was if Hunters switched people's attention from just looking at ties in a one-dimensional manner to being given a technology experience that was related to ties, and in doing so creating a relationship of trust between browser and website.

We have since gone on to upgrade LuxuryTies by adding video. The idea behind the total integration of product brand and technology within the website package we now offer was once put in a very succinct manner:

> Your knowledge of what you do needs to be two foot wide and two miles deep for your product sector, showing that you can reach way beyond all the others, who are just two miles wide and a shallow two inches deep when you start drilling them down.

As we were offering the capability to exercise choice in an enjoyable and novel way with information direct from Hunters – Savile Row's Master Silk Tie Maker – we could do more than many traditional stores. We were able to add a greater depth of visual capability and information for the user and deliver the message as to what the Hunters' specialist tie brand is all about through the interaction with our site visitors in our virtual dressing rooms.

CHAPTER 7

Using technology to develop key brand factors

Trust is, in our opinion, the true secret behind a brand. As the brand itself becomes a respected authority in its field so people trust that it will always be acceptable (in our case to wear). With the search engines delivering us in the top ten results we found that people were tending to trust the sites in the higher positions before the lower ones – the browser/searcher premise being that if you aren't in the top ten you aren't any good.

We have to assume that the search engines and directories are their markets' respected authorities. Many of us do not question the results they return, and this forms the first part of our on-line brand trust equation. The second is the website's innovation and the third is the quality and authenticity of a unique product that is not widely available.

Knowing and understanding the concept of a brand as containing a series of tangible and intangible elements (see Figure 7.1 overleaf), we realized that through the use of engaging technology, the media and the engineered communication of our uniqueness a trust between consumer and website can and does evolve before the website user takes physical ownership of the product. Once the trust factor has been established this should lead to a purchase decision based on the brand's credentials alone.

Hunters – Brand Factors

❋ Credentials: Savile Row – all user groups

❋ Personality: Englishness

❋ Media: endorsements

❋ Consumer message: alter to user groups

❋ Product: unique high-quality offering

Average brand building cost: $1 billion (source: *Competing for the Future*)

Figure 7.1 The main concepts of branding.

In many ways the element of enjoyment (making someone laugh) is a key feature in our website's ability to gain trust, and if you are able to create a measure of enjoyment from using your website so you will find that people will continue to recommend you to others.

There are other supporting messages that must be delivered and that we have identified in our graduate business school research on this subject (also shown in Figure 7.1). After reading through the list of the Hunters' brand factors we expect that you will be able to replace ours with your own as you start to think how your brand will be portrayed on-line and the key features you will concentrate on to add value to your uniqueness. These are the key areas we focus on and promote to our website users to gain their confidence and trust in an on-line relationship that we want to develop quickly.

The browser/searcher message

The 'consumer message' is perhaps our last key feature before we show you how we identified uniqueness and found our brand's position relative to our markets and competitors.

As the search engines and directories are the initial consumers of information regarding your website – what you have for sale/on offer – the message you use to describe your website has to be adapted to meet the varying browser groups at different levels across international markets.

Optimization can go some way to achieving this, but we would point out that the end must justify the means, and that what you are selling/offering is what you say it is and will fit in with a want/lifestyle need which is met by your brand's value-added proposition.

Brands meet lifestyle needs in both business and personal purchasing. People like to own or control a brand product or service. For example, a manager would rather be put in charge of one of the big five management consultancies' project teams than a team from an unknown consultancy. The inference here is that controlling or owning a valuable resource gives the manager status among their immediate peer group and looks good on their CV.

The key brand-influencing factors for Hunters via LuxuryTies may be summarized as follows:

- Localized target media – winning media that are relevant to the sector.

- Interactive on-line presence – people are actually given a reason to visit the website before other competitor sites.

- Enjoyment – people like the presentation protocols and enjoy playing with the website's choice capabilities.

- Knowledge depth – we are the category leader through our ability to share relevant authentic information through streaming video, choice capabilities, etc. We also show our faces through the streaming media.

- Visibility – we get to know our markets and get involved with them, such as giving in-store presentations.

- Regular website updating – we keep reinventing the site with new add-ons that increase user knowledge, their capability with the product and experience, leading the field in the product/service class.

- Watching the competition – technology is not the complete answer. The market for new innovation continues to advance – we have to make sure what we have is state-of-the-art.

Whatever the message you employ in the promotion of your website, it must encapsulate your uniqueness in at least one clear and coherent sentence, or it will be lost. Always avoid using long words and remember, although English is a widely spoken and understood language, technical English is difficult – keep it simple.

The internet is global. People from all over the world will be looking at your site. Why put them off by trying to look and sound like a professor? The real experts make the complex seem easy to understand and in doing so win acclaim.

We are going to focus in detail on creating the consumer message for the home page later. For now you must start to think about your own brand message and test it on your target buyer/browser for their first response. Also consider how you will develop a series of brand protocols that can be communicated quickly and concisely.

Positioning your value-added brand to the market

By now you will have come to understand that brands are far more subtle than just names and logos – they give people status and meet the aspirational needs of ownership. The winning brands are continually in demand. They are their markets' trusted authorities, with accepted yet unwritten and universally regarded credentials. Above all, they are their product/sector specialists. (It should be noted that brands have a recurring habit of out-performing the stock markets. In the luxury brand sector alone their returns are some of the highest year on year.)

As brands are representative of a total product/marketing message, the best brands are supported by superior marketing and advertising which over a number of years has established them as leaders in their sector – how can you even begin to go about creating one, let alone becoming one on-line?

If we add to this the fact that brands themselves have 'personalities' then we have quite a challenge on our hands to express this on-line and through the search engines in a few simple words.

On-line the best supplying company might not be regarded as 'the best' due to a poor search engine ranking position. To a degree, the search engines decide which websites get returned first depending on the site's own optimization skill, so that an unknown brand might get purchased or have its site visited more than a known brand if it is seen more often following a generic product-specific search.

The question we asked ourselves was: 'when two products (one branded the other non-branded) that both satisfy the same purpose are placed side by side, why is the branded product purchased more often than the non-branded?'

This question continues to perplex brand marketers – no one has ever come up with the full answer. The beauty (or desire for ownership) is in the eye of the purchaser of the brand against the non-branded product and it is difficult to judge what a consumer is going to do from one hour to the next.

Despite this, accountants still tend to imagine that sales and consumers are controlled by a magical tap that can be turned on and off at will, with no regard to the real conditions in the world that contribute to a consumer's behaviour or their purchase criteria in relation to their changing needs and aspirations.

We decided during our research that some websites were themselves evolving as brands. We want LuxuryTies to evolve as a site known for Savile Row quality men's accessory items through its innovative technological capabilities specific to ties represented by the Hunters' brand.

However, it is easier to say this than it has been to achieve it. We had to turn back to our graduate business school research, where we examined the creation of niche brands and the differentiation tactics that can be used to design a product that meets a segment of the market and which is thereafter calibrated as a brand specific to the segment and has a revenue-earning potential.

During our empirical research we came up with a concept that we named the brand staircase, as shown in Figure 7.2. This went some way to assisting us in designing niche products and websites.

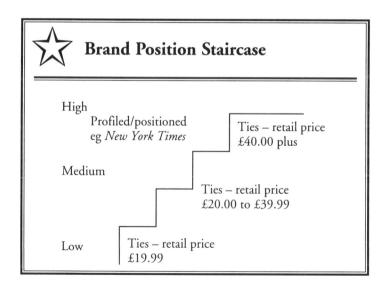

Figure 7.2 The brand staircase.

Initially the staircase showed us that the tie market tends to be segmented by price from the lowest to the highest just like products in most markets. Another example here could be cars, where the basic model is at the foot of the stairs and at the head is the top of the range car with all the extras which is the most expensive.

As purchasers move up the staircase through ownership factors personal to them (graduating out of one brand or product class into the next) so additional benefits are added to the product as a result of the brand increasing the ownership status, eg creating subtle differentiators that are visible against competitor offerings. These differentiators are then communicated in a lifestyle message. In many instances the message is a visual image of a lifestyle enhancement, the idea being 'to aspire is to own'.

We applied the staircase concept to our ties back in 1996 and then to our website in 1999/2000. In both cases, once we had understood what was different about all the other brand ties and our competitors' websites, we were able to learn what could and would be unique about Hunters and LuxuryTies and where our niche was going to be. This is the process of product differentiation in its simplest form.

We have always felt that it is better to be the leader in a niche (ie a small segment of the total market), as the market is narrower and the cost of servicing and meeting that segment lower, rather than trying to meet the total market. Using this tactic it is possible for an unknown company to emerge as a brand far sooner, especially if you have first-mover advantage – and providing of course the market wants what you are offering!

To occupy your own niche is to have a level of control over your market that any new entrant will find difficult to emulate, enabling you to interact with your market on a more personal basis as you have control and are the trusted authority.

The difficult task is searching for and locating a market niche for your differentiated products/service which you have room to grow over time. (Our research on this appears in later chapters.)

Hunters operates within a mature, highly competitive market and as a brand is a relative newcomer, but with the use of the brand staircase we were able to create noticeable differences between ourselves and our competitors' offerings, having reviewed other products/websites against our own. Some call this 'brand engineering' – we prefer to call it 'brand inspiration' as we were able to reintroduce elements of a tie that had been forgotten since automated production methods were introduced into our sector many years ago.

The research we applied in developing our ties was also applied to developing the LuxuryTies website. For example, the lower priced tie websites tend to talk first about how cheap their prices are, whereas more expensive tie websites focus their visitors away from price and on to their company's origins and credentials.

As you look at how and what your competitors are 'offering' you can locate where you can deliver uniqueness, on the basis of why what you have is of value and why you are better than others. Following this test you should be able to position yourselves on a staircase particular to your market after having applied your differentiators.

Once you know where you are, you'll know what you have to do to be better and can begin to structure your credentials and the messages that support the unique capability offering of your brand product website to the market niche you hope to engage.

By now you should understand the basic principles of brand engineering and development and what a brand needs to contain. Also you should be able to identify how and why some brands have been successful and many others have failed. Research statistics state that over 97% of all new brands don't make it out of the marketing department as the marketers are unable to lock into their target consumers' subconscious code as to why that product or service will be of value to them. As is often the case the company doesn't know how to explain and deliver the benefits of ownership of its product, though this is becoming more and more difficult today due to the universal nature of an on-line multicultural audience.

The additional value-added benefits you create can, if designed and packaged correctly, greatly increase your chances of developing a brand position within a splinter niche market where consumers will derive the main benefit from your website.

Following the principle of the staircase you should write down your five main on-line competitors and make a critical evaluation of their differentiators. You then design your own site where you see a gap that, if filled, can give value to your website's visitors and thus create customers.

However, you must decide where you want to be in your market – low/middle/high – and focus on just one part. Do not attempt to meet the needs of the whole spectrum as consumers tend to dismiss the 'one message fits all' theory.

High rankings to protect value-added uniqueness

One aspect of e-commerce is certain – whatever you do and no matter how unique you think you are in doing it there is always competition. The focus of the critical issue for Hunters then branched out to encompass how, if we could get high rankings for the generic term, we could then protect, maintain and build on our position.

If we think back to those 13 million plus other websites that have yet to make any money, it seems to us that they failed to identify what would be critical in their business model when it came to understanding who their customers were going to be and why they should even use the new website aimed at them.

Following on from this, we have to ask where they are in relation to their market and how they were going to convert whatever it was they were doing into an engaging message and then into a sustainable revenue stream.

As we look back at many of the now failed e-businesses that were operational at the time of our research, in most instances these organizations were not sales led. They believed that the technology alone (and other organization brands at knock-down prices) would be enough to carry them through if supported by high advertising.

Fundamentally, you cannot just tell a person you are a brand, or generate discussion groups to talk about the benefits of your product and service. Experience is the required factor and on-line the experience has to be pre-purchase, as a browser cannot hold or inspect the product in their hands before divulging their credit card details to an unknown organization 5,000 miles away.

This is why trust (and the other credentials mentioned earlier) is needed and one of the key credentials is being returned in the top ten.

The technical route may be viable if you are a search engine or a software application provider that people need in their life, but it is pointless if you are selling a tangible product or service into a mature market. Coupled with this is the fact that to make a 'go' of the business would require funding beyond the gross national product of some countries, as well as everyone in the world buying something from you three times each year.

Throughout our own site development we believed that sales and a focus on a strong customer brand experience would be the main emphasis, bundled together with enjoyable interactive website value-added protocols. In undertaking our research we realized that the critical issue that faced us was that, with no money to undertake a marketing action, we would have to make the search engines and directories work for us.

At the end of our research period (February 2000) we had redefined our original issue analysis and created a new sub-issue list that comprised the following:

- Identify the search engines/directories that our profiled consumer is most likely to visit and employ a concentration strategy aimed at these engines/directories to ensure LuxuryTies would respond to generic term searches on them. We decided we would rather be Number 1 on just one search engine than number 90 on five search engines/directories.

- Summarize a Hunters' brand message that is more compelling than that of competitors to entice visitors in. And convert those visitors into customers by giving them a pre-purchase brand experience through technology that is lifestyle focused, that generates trust and that unlocks the subconscious codes of what Savile Row is about.

- Evaluate a defensive process to protect b2b and b2c customers and throw off competition.

- Identify which organizations are pouring money into advertising our product class and to which engines and directories that money is going.

Once this list was created and we had the relevant knowledge, we realized that the issue of zero finance would fade as we piggy-backed on the major organizations' attempts to promote themselves to a wider market in their efforts to generate immediate revenues to justify their VC's investment.

Our on-line competitors continually fought for market share above our heads. We could easily see where they spent money promoting existing brands on-line that were freely available from a number of off-line and on-line channels, drawing in our target customer who would view LuxuryTies through our message of an alternative unique technology application, providing we were returned in the same generic product search results set.

Effectively, by being in the top ten results for a product class, we could redirect a browser's attention away from the original advertiser who had induced the search in the first place. In gauging where the money from the bigger funded companies was going, we were then able to calibrate a one page e-commerce market direction finder that would support Hunters' LuxuryTies website when it was launched two months later.

We were continually scanning the web for opening leads, focusing on ten of our competitors' websites for our product class, watching how they were attracting visitors through their promotions at certain times and the type of brands and price points they were moving in and out of. This was the equivalent of an off-line marketing exercise where you size up the competition before you make a move. However, on-line it is much easier and less costly, as the research is being done from home.

Innovation pulls in the press

From the launch in April 2000 onwards the novelty value and experience of using LuxuryTies to select and buy ties was reported on by the media globally (not only in Tulsa!) generating headlines such as:

'From Savile Row To Cyber Row'
> (*Better Business*, June 2000, focusing
> on our e-commerce developments)

'Where the Shirts are Scanned, Not Stuffed'
> (Warren Hoge, *New York Sunday Times*,
> April 2000, when we launched the site)

Winning quality reviews in media that are focused at our target market has the tendency to endorse our brand's credentials and LuxuryTies' ability to go further than all the other tie and accessory websites.

The media are a very powerful influencer, and we have never underestimated their capability in promoting Hunters and LuxuryTies, but the media will always check the message you are presenting to them. They have a duty to their readers to verify all copy at source, something the pure hype e-businesses have never been able to take on board, thinking a one-page press release is all it's going to take to get a newspaper to write about them! (Interestingly enough we found that such PR has an increased visitor value of three weeks, after which time the site traffic returns to its normal level.)

Summary

In this section of the book, we have focused on why brands are more than just logos or names (although there are plenty who have lost millions trying to prove the opposite) as brands speak to people and can inspire them. Now we can begin to understand where and how optimization can be used in the process of brand establishment.

Both the name Hunters and its website create thoughts of the England of days gone by. It is authentic and locks into its target market's subconscious coding when Savile Row is used to describe a level of clothing quality. Other names have also emerged on-line that create such an impression via their unique branded quality products/services, which are particular to the organization selling/presenting them and are not likely to be traded down as a result of price or mass availability.

Some significant added value must be created by the website that is real in near physical terms and that, like uniqueness itself, is not available elsewhere. In short you have to create a difference between your organization and your competitors', and ensure that it cannot be emulated. This is known as differentiation, and it must be delivered in a novel and enjoyable manner that excites the audience and makes them sit up and say 'wow, this is good fun'.

In today's world you do not want to be perceived as boring. This is a common fault among millions of websites, all hoping that their free offers or cheap prices will be enough to attract a customer. Creativity through technological innovation can be a real hook and the browser's attention can be caught and held for a time while they inspect and examine what you offer – providing the novelty value of using your site goes beyond the home page.

We sometimes wonder how many of the old-timer CEOs ever realize the value of their organizations' advertising to other smaller companies such as ours waiting patiently in the wings, watching them all the time. (Their efforts in trying to develop new markets have never actually been wasted, and we do have a lot to thank many of them for!) Do they even stop and consider that they have created secondary markets that are more profitable for companies like Hunters to cash in on than the ones they were trying to develop?

Perhaps this is the beauty of being a small business. Response to market lead-times are shorter, and with the continued cost reduction in e-commerce the time needed to create a multimedia-enabled, highly functional website and 'cash in' on emerging secondary niche markets (even today) can be much shorter, as the smaller organization lacks the hierarchy and mindset of its bigger 'same market' counterpart.

All it will take for you to overcome the critical issue in developing sales is to locate where your profiled customer visits, and then organize all your activities around that market – first the search engine/database in a concentrated approach, and then your customer, giving them the trust and enjoyment they need to buy from you as an unknown.

Study and think about where and why the big players advertise and what levels and type of message they employ. From there you should be able to think up a better message that is focused towards the spin-off market being quietly created that will meet a segment of the total user group which wants the more unique offering that you can give.

In applying the staircase model, you should be able to position yourself to the segment of the market that is of interest to your organization (or where you feel a gap currently exists) and explain to your visitors why you are a better proposition than the others. If you have been returned in the top ten results set for a generic search you are already creating credibility for your e-business in the eyes of the browser community.

You have to remember that pure technological innovation alone will not protect your business and markets – you have to seek out other ways that will move you towards your goal through value-added product benefits and experiences to deliver the important brand factor of trust through an engaging experience.

If you can create and thereafter isolate a unique feature of your website/product offering that is attractive to visitors, this will form the foundation for your value-added experience, enhancing the user's ability and leading to the evolution and acceptance of your brand's credential set.

Thereafter, by applying the concepts of concentrated market identification, any high ranking position you gain through optimization will focus your site towards the search engines' and directories' target audience who search under generic phrases specific to your products/services.

This in itself will establish your website presence as an authority, on the basis that your organization's knowledge and added value is deeper than that of your competitors. In turn, this will enable more visitors to see and understand what your company does and learn/understand why you are just as (if not more) unique than the bigger organizations who won't stop spending on traditional advertising in the vain attempt to create brands that have no substance.

You have to make sure you don't make the same mistakes that these funded old-boy management start-ups made, by trying to apply traditional off-line managerial concepts and theories that only worked within great sprawling organizations, where the benefits were never really felt anyway.

Your thoughts must be like your brand – unique and innovative. And remember that wisdom is gained through knowledge, not years.

PART 3

Branding for the on-line customer

CHAPTER 8

Optimizing towards the customer

Be close to your customers or else!

It's not the candy store (website), it's the plot of land (search engine position) it's built on that's worth the real money. How true!

We always try to communicate with our customers in a very novel and entertaining way, never talking down to them or pushing them, preferring to play a small part within the market itself rather than being an external supplier to it. However, many of the website home pages we came across during our early research tended to put themselves in the supplier category by employing one or more of the following opening propositions:

- 'Welcome to the Home of [eg] Shoelaces'

- '50% Off Our Shoelaces'

- 'Immediate Shoelace Delivery – Free'

- We Are the Web's No. 1 Shoelace Supplier'

All that these statements do is identify a website as being 'the same as the rest'.

It's a continuing and sad fact of internet life that most home pages give out the same old message, time after time. When really, it just takes a little creative thought to put something together that's going to be catchy enough to encourage a browser to take a look at what you're about. There's no harm in trying to make contact with your visitor on a more personal basis.

We deliver a lot of lectures and keynote speeches on business matters (particularly e-branding) and one of the first (and best) lessons we were given when it came to being a guest speaker was that you should say something at the outset that is going to identify you with your audience and make them sit up and take notice. This is what those 'same as the other' websites fail to achieve.

One reason for this lack of customer closeness or the 'non sit up factor' rests with many of the old-boy CEOs, who believed that they would still be miles away from real customers, acting and operating just as they did at their ex-employer where a customer was referred to broadly as an anonymous third-party entity called 'sales'. So the new CEOs distanced themselves immediately from what the new on-line business was all about.

Because their ex-employer didn't have to do too much to win customers, many felt that it wasn't their role or responsibility when they ended up at the funded dotcoms. As far as they were concerned their remit was to create an organization with a framework from which all this could develop.

But if you don't get the message right on day one, what's the point? And if you can't identify your business with your customers' needs because you are too busy looking at a really clever accounting package (or some other distraction that's suddenly really important) then there's just no chance of the business doing any business.

Of course, these CEOs had customer care departments or call centres at their ex-employers and were bringing these departments into the newly funded dotcoms (to really wind the customer up). As long as there was someone somewhere that called a customer a customer that end of the business was 'secured' and this satisfied them and the VCs – another box ticked.

With that mentality, it's no surprise that many of the promising funded start-ups have gone out of business. The whole idea of the internet was to do things differently with a new organizational culture, not just to replicate old off-line working habits/practices and systems that we all hate (call centres).

There's nothing worse than making a customer feel like they are being processed or 'just a number', but most of the big funded dotcoms did just that. Everything was clinical and didn't relate to the customer or even purport to have the customer's best interests at heart.

However, the perception that a customer could be processed was firmly rooted in the CEOs' mindsets and when they moved to the funded start-ups they convinced the dotcoms to act in the same way, regarding customers as the second lowest form of human life (the first being investors) as they set about working on ways to fleece even more out of both groups. Although many didn't win any customers, they certainly had won the VCs over, who layed it all off on to the shareholders.

Why? Because most newly funded start-ups truly believed their user and customer base would be global, especially with all that advertising. They just couldn't fail.

The reality, though, wasn't like that. Yet it could have been if the approach towards customers had been different, or at least sincere in that the e-business had the customers' total interests at heart and wanted to interact with them in some beneficial way instead of trying to sell them hyped-up junk.

Today we are all wise to what has happened (as usual after the event). Legal claims are now being made by shareholders against management teams for what's beginning to look like some of the most elaborate cases of corporate skullduggery ever conceived.

To some extent the power is gradually reverting back to the customer and the business founders, through the customer choice factor and inspirational ideas that the new entrepreneurs have brought to the world of commerce.

In the vast majority of cases the only reason some of us feel as if we still don't have a great deal of choice is that many of the new big funded dotcoms still act like the old off-line businesses from which we are trying to escape. (This is not surprising really as that's where most of the management ability originates.)

There was and is nothing new about them although their hype tried to tell us there was, but it was (as always) the customers or the browsers who decided whether or not the new website met its promise and goals, and not the management team's credibility.

However, some great businesses have emerged, as stated in Part 2, who really know what choice is all about and give us the new choice capability we as consumers all want.

Mainly these truly great organizations are still to some extent in the hands of their founders, many of whom have not been tainted by the industries' so called leaders (or conditioned as to how and what to do within the new economy organizations) as the functions and roles at the start-ups were not a place for a career manager to replicate their old off-line 'skills'.

The whim factor

Another problem for the CEO in the new start-up was a total lack of customer information/profiling data, and as they didn't know who the customer was likely to be, a fear of the unknown set in. Hence more issue avoidance tactics were put into place.

The new CEO carried on applying the same old management techniques in the newly funded business (mostly issue avoidance) while the VC's cash continued to diminish through its allocation to whatever new whim or 'project' fascinated the CEO.

What the new CEO just didn't reckon on was that without the buffers normally available to them at their old companies (in terms of rows of middle and junior managers to protect them) any decision made could have a pretty quick effect and this would be shown in the sales – or the lack of them. So the buck stopped with the CEO, a position they were not at all used to.

CEOs are like chairmen – they both suffer from whims that are often the result of what he or she has read or heard about at some spurious two-day residential 'top management' seminar (networking event) costing £2,500, at a very grand hotel with an equally grand black tie gala dinner on the last night.

After the seminar these CEOs strut back to their organizations full of bright ideas or whims (and expensive wine) that are next to impossible to implement as they depend on the customer buying into the new 'wonder' strategy or tactic which is so complex that no one has understood it.

The end result is that the employees become confused by the introduction of these new words and concepts that bring about a directional change in the business's original strategy, which was usually to sell or deliver something in a very simple and enjoyable way.

Once this situation has arisen both the management and the employees become totally confused. This is compounded with pressure – the pressure being to make the new whim work as all the eggs are now in one basket!

The trouble was – and for many still is – the new strategy didn't work out, because three months later the CEO was at a different seminar, learning even more new and mind-blowing things which served only to question and replace what was dreamed up at the last seminar.

By now the CEO has also become a bit confused, leading to agitation and frustration. So even more new outlandish ideas are introduced to offset the CEO's sheer lack of understanding as they keep searching for solutions that don't involve the customer.

While all this was going on the funded start-up kept moving away from its customers. We have seen this many times before: when things are really bad in businesses (and it's normally because sales are poor) the management turns to the organization's internal areas in an attempt to try and defend their own inability by laying the blame on the employees (or in many cases the founders).

Gradually the CEOs begin to switch allegiance from the organization to the VCs. Their new role of developing a more robust business model or sorting out the problem staff that they had inherited is justified by the claim that, once completed, it will right what is wrong.

But 'sorting out' costs money, as this means redundancies – not 'firings' as the CEO calls it in the lunchtime slang to the yes-men they introduced as managers to the funded start-up.

Suddenly everyone's attention is turned away from the critical issue of zero or poor sales. The employees live in fear (which is understandable as many will lose their jobs) and the talk of the entire organization centres on redundancy. Suddenly new strategies, concepts and – as always – customers are forgotten while the witch-hunt gets underway to find the person or department to blame for the disaster or the CEO's lack of ability.

Now sales begin to collapse (that's if they were lucky enough to have had any) and the whole ship takes a heavy list. The business can't sustain itself, all the in-fighting is wrecking the place and people start to realize that because the start-up was too big in the first place it could only survive while the VCs were at hand to bale it out while everyone (including the CEO) was waiting for customers to bite.

Ultimately the start-up collapses – all because the guy at the top failed to reach out to the customer, to identify the business and its range of brand products/services and to concentrate on their customers' needs.

Today we read about the closures of companies that were around when we started on-line and which we thought would be the organizations of the future. It is sad that many potential start-ups could have succeeded if they focused on their customers' direct needs. If their CEOs had spent as much time thinking about customers as they did about their stock options many of these businesses would still be around today.

Marketing via optimization

In the US a waistcoat is known as a 'vest', so if you are selling waistcoats there make sure your content contains text particular to the language of the market you are attempting to engage.

In the past we have won business by finding out the word for 'ties' in another language and using it. Optimize your site using words/phrases as if you yourself were looking for what you offer, and check out the market through research across as many generic translations for your product/service as possible.

Most website designers and builders 'don't do optimization', mainly because it's a marketing process that is not in their remit. Many build great websites, but what's the point if it never gets a visit, or the company has to spend money promoting the web address? The best sales are those where the customer has found you.

You should by now realize the importance and benefits of low-cost optimization, as an alternative approach to expensive advertising, to promote a website (and how some brand positioning can be attained through this process). We are now going to begin applying the principles introduced to you in previous chapters by developing a framework in which to create a marketing and website branding programme for your e-business.

Following your review of this section you will come to understand that there are a number of existing built-in marketing elements available on your current (or planned) website that can be used to generate high ranking positions and engage focused browser traffic. This can be achieved through the synchronization of your home page (which the browser sees) and the programming behind it (which the search engine or directory see).

You will be introduced to a simple way of collecting browser data to give you a future benefit/advantage. We will also be analyzing and adapting common marketing messages that have been used off-line but which may also be used successfully on-line, after some slight alterations following our experience-based rationale.

At this stage it is important to consider another myth that cost us a lot of time – the difference between on-line and off-line buyers – as this forms the underlying basis for our targeted market approach. Even today many commentators try to establish two distinct customer types: on-line buyers and off-line buyers.

Often myths like this (and the one about $89 per customer) are a form of defensive marketing used by the bigger companies to scare off new market entrants. They try to convince us that their markets are difficult to enter and survive in as there's a new breed of consumer that can only be engaged in a certain way and the route to finding that way takes years of research and so on.

We read over and over in the financial press and company prospectuses information about how complex markets are and have become. However, let us also remember that markets are all driven by consumers of some kind who either like or don't like what you do – where's the complexity in that?

Terms like 'matrix market business models' are just more managerial speak that's designed to put off small e-businesses, while other defensive statements are also used to protect an organization's markets. However, the more a company shouts about how complicated its business is the more interested we get – normally it isn't complex but a scam designed to throw us off the scent.

The reality is that consumers on- and off-line are the same people – there's no difference to their mindset. What is important to them off-line is just as important to them on-line. However, it is the case that some people are not prepared to part with credit card details on-line or simply prefer to buy their goods off-line. Maybe that's all there is to the 'big' difference – a matter of confidence.

Realistically, all that has changed for the consumer is that on-line the exercise of choice has been widened by an unknown amount, depending on the sector of the market from which they are buying.

Effectively consumers are already trained in many product credentials. For example, they know what a tie is, what it's used for and when it should be used.

Once we had accepted this we decided there was no point in trying to alter completely a fundamental or existing product message. For example, we could not tell people that ties are actually also useful as a substitute for a belt to hold one's trousers up as the underlying message of what a tie does is already embedded in a person's mind. But many new start-up e-businesses felt they could rewrite a product's primary use, when really they should have created co-relationships between their products and others, developing or enhancing a new use where that 'new added value' could be delivered on-line.

As an existing product such as a tie cannot be given a new function, we felt that what we *could* do was build on a consumer's existing knowledge of products and services, underpinning this with a few new phrases that encapsulate our uniqueness and drawing browsers/visitors in on supporting messages as to why we are unique and why our website should be entered. In effect we were going to show what LuxuryTies could do for them that another website couldn't. To achieve this, we began by making sure the description tag that accompanied our website at the search engines/directories made us stand out from the crowd by coining the following phrase:

'To tie or knot to silk tie a necktie. Hunters Savile Row's Master Silk Tie Maker.'

A small borrowing from Mr W Shakespeare, but catchy enough to engage our audience who like to think a bit more about their clothing. Our description tag reached out through its Englishness and eccentricity, while differentiating us from all the rest with the words 'Savile Row'.

We know that, fundamentally, the products at the end of the pipeline are pretty much the same in terms of functionality. However, today it is the purchasing channel, or mechanism that people use to buy, that has changed and will continue to do so. Therefore more thought and personality has to be employed throughout the whole project to give LuxuryTies a lift in the eyes of a potential customer.

We said earlier that consumers are becoming smarter in their use of technology. The same applies to the messages that are put over by brands with their supporting products. Consumers know when they are being sold 'a line', they know which messages are false and which are true. It's the credentials behind you and the trust or enjoyment bond that create consumer confidence – and that's the difference between a 'buy' or 'forget it' decision.

For example, Savile Row means gentlemen's clothing wherever you are in the world. But it's the fact that Hunters make ties in Savile Row that gives our brand fundamental credence without even having to use the words clothes or ties, and it is this location that also starts off the relationship of trust between the browser/visitor and the LuxuryTies website.

In your analysis to establish credibility you will have found which messages engage your market. They should reinforce your uniqueness and, having applied the brand staircase model, you will have identified the significant differentiators pertinent to your product or service that will meet a niche or segment of your total market.

You should then be able to express these in relation to what the rest of the market is saying about similar products and provide a more focused value-added proposition. For example, 'company X performs the basic role, but we increase and enhance this with such and such additional features which benefit the consumer in the following ways …'

We are going to apply these and other practices to your own situation in the following pages to demonstrate:

- the importance of the home page

- 'brand by association' tactics – the importance of being seen among the market leaders and in the right places

- segmenting the market by user types

- identifying potential markets

- marketing through generic term optimization.

By the end you will be able to select a segment of your total market, deliver a compelling home page message to that area of the market and understand how basic optimization within a brand creation programme can be applied.

Promoting your on-line brand

Your browser's attention span is about eight seconds long, and within this time you have to tell them why they should enter your site, regard you as credible, understand what it is you do that's better than all the rest and – most importantly – buy what you have on offer.
Figure 8.1 summarizes the task ahead.

Sales and Marketing

Cyberspace promotion:

❋ Use of on-line methods

❋ Traditional PR still the best

❋ Managing a brand on-line

❋ Channel conflict

❋ On-line competition

Figure 8.1 Promoting your on-line brand.

Use of on-line methods – engaging the browser via the home page

Website marketing has its own issues, in particular the importance of the home page as a key influencer to draw in the visitor. You can apply traditional advertising to tell people a website address relating to the product or service you supply in the hope they will visit – but that's an expensive way to create a market that might just not be there.

Really we are always going to be better off promoting through the search engines with a fully optimized home page and getting the rankings to put us in a top position for what we offer, alongside those who have paid the advertising agencies to generate the market in the first place.

We can draw in the 'promotion' aspect of the '4Ps' (the old marketing gambit of product, place, price and promotion) if we regard our home page (normally the first page of a website) as part of our 'advertising' that will act as an inducer for a browser to enter our site once they have selected us from the results set returned. They will hopefully have selected us from the results set due to a combination of seeing us in a top ten position and having read our catchy search engine/directory description tag.

Earlier chapters will have helped you realize that brand marketing itself is far more subtle than just a logo. To be a brand the name itself must represent trust, deep product knowledge and personality – and now through optimization our aim is to get all of that into our home page to engage a potential customer who is searching for what we are selling.

Our LuxuryTies site visitors regard us as credible for a number of specific reasons. We hope they say to themselves that having viewed and experienced our on-line uniqueness, they might just be tempted to buy one of our ties, and then come back again, ultimately making Hunters their number one choice brand for ties through all that we deliver to them.

In understanding and accepting this as our goal we can start to do what is required, such as being seen in the right place, saying the right things and in fact being our customers' friend. That's what we want – an immediate trust-based relationship delivered in a few short sentences as we begin to identify our website to our browsers'/visitors' needs.

At this stage it is worth taking a look at a typical browser route map, which is how we all find websites (in this case ones selling shoelaces) and the common pitfalls that arise (see Figure 8.2).

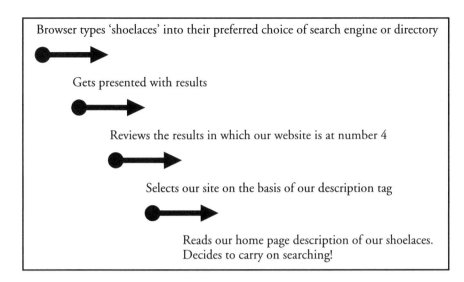

Browser types 'shoelaces' into their preferred choice of search engine or directory

Gets presented with results

Reviews the results in which our website is at number 4

Selects our site on the basis of our description tag

Reads our home page description of our shoelaces. Decides to carry on searching!

Figure 8.2 Typical browser route map.

There are a number of reasons for a browser not entering your site. The most common is that the home page message (text or image) fails to grab the browser's immediate attention and reach out to their subconscious codes – you must know why browsers/searchers are looking at your site and what their expectations are.

As the home page is the first page a browser sees it is like the cover of a book – if it's too boring it won't get picked off the shelf.

Your aim is to create and control a browser's mindset from the start, by writing an introduction to your website that is so enticing that the browser will be compelled to go further on and will (after having read your website home page) be thinking along the lines you are presenting.

This itself is also an area of optimization. Optimization falls into two parts: the first is the text on your home page and the second is the elements of the programming behind the home page itself.

Looking at Figure 8.2, and assuming that your shoelace website has been returned in the top results for your product class, to get a browser/searcher this far and then lose them on the basis of a poorly constructed home page is both a massive waste of effort and a lost opportunity.

The issues for you as a website brand marketer are that you have to give people a reason to look at your site once they have found it, especially as the bigger brands only have to apply their name, or if they are particularly well known, their logo.

The constraints for you as an 'unknown' company are that you do not yet have the brand credentials of trust, as the market probably doesn't even know you exist. Therefore you have to create a message that's stronger than all the household names.

Further, on a home page you are restricted with regard to the visuals (pictures, use of flash graphics etc) as we have a browser time factor working against us – no one waits that long for a page to download.

That's the bad news. The good news is that in reading and thinking about the earlier chapters in this book you should have begun to identify a number of features from your product or service that make you unique to your market. The question is, how can we get these key elements over quickly and in a very simple way that draws in the visitor, who accepts us as a suitable alternative, and ultimately converts into sales?

CHAPTER 9

The role of the home page in brand optimization

Home page optimized content

We look at many website home pages and they give us no reason to go further than the first two sentences – that's if we have waited long enough for some of them to download!

The home page, as stated, is the start of the optimization process and, as you will read later, features such as key word stuffing (using the same word over and over on either your home page or within the programming) may get you banned by a search engine and directories.

Therefore you have to limit the times you employ a certain word(s) that is pertinent to your product/service. (This is just one of the many rules that professional optimization accommodates.)

Earlier we discussed the establishment of the brand credential set. This now comes into play as you realize that, as a purely promotional tactic, it is best to be seen among similar brands that are well known since this can give you near equal status.

For example, Hunters in its b2b model has to be seen alongside the other famous brand names in an off-line store so as to give the brand name Hunters credibility, and on-line in the results set returned to a browser LuxuryTies/Hunters has to be seen alongside the other famous brand names.

This is perhaps the most difficult aspect of a brand manager's brief. We identified our market through the differential analysis and lifestyle questionnaires over a period of time. The internet globalizes Hunters via LuxuryTies and as our brand becomes better known around the world so we alter or rearrange the credential set to fit different target consumer groups and their subconscious codes/needs.

For example, in Italy the name Savile Row is very important in the purchasing decision, whereas in the USA 'Made in England' is just as widely accepted as Savile Row. All we do through our home page is alter the optimization to the market we are targeting, depending on which engine and directory we are promoting LuxuryTies to, eg an Italian-specific engine.

We have to ensure that we know our search engines and directories (which we do through research) and we have to ensure that we do not become listed in the wrong category. (That happens to a lot of websites when their owners/operators use a low quality multiple submission software tool.)

If we found that we had become listed/indexed alongside refrigerators we would have failed in our optimization tactic of being seen alongside the main brand supplier base for our product and there would be a lot of lost opportunities, possibly even sales.

Home page constraints

Some IT consultants suggest you optimize your website with your competitors' brand names (in the computer programming part behind the home page) so as to be returned in the same results set. For example, when someone performs a search for, say, Rolls Royce, among the results returned appears 'Dave's Autos for Quality Second-Hand Used Cars', as Dave's site's programming is stuffed with the keyword 'Rolls Royce'.

We do not recommend this tactic as it is ripping off another organization and will undoubtedly get you into trouble with the search engine/directory. This is a type of spam that could result in your domain name/website being delisted or banned altogether.

Another home page related brand development challenge is that in the off-line world a brand/product performs at alternative prices as local economies require organizations to price tactically. (This means it is more expensive in one country than in another – a good example being car prices in Continental Europe, which are 30% cheaper than they are in the UK for the same model.)

One way around this is to operate a number of different locally hosted websites for the same brand/product at 'the price the market will bear' in a number of foreign languages so as to appear local to the market. An alternative is to create a website with foreign language translation capabilities in terms of pricing, message, style, etc.

The last option is in our opinion the best – working on the premise that, as the website stays under the complete control of your organization, consistency is ensured throughout, and because it fits well with the practice of limiting the supplier base to protect a brand.

So if a policy of the same or like pricing is pursued across international markets, conflicts in the price/trust brand message are avoided – providing your branded product does not become cheaper elsewhere as a result of it being repackaged and sold on by a third-party website/channel.

Your home page is the shop window of your website and summarizes your product/service and your unique value-added proposition, while giving consideration to:

- delivering a better proposition to your browser group than the main brands for the same product class

- presenting the essence of your message in multiple languages (if required) as quickly as possible

- replacing the fact that you might be the cheapest source on the web with another equally important factor(s) that can outweigh price in terms of buyer or customer benefit

- developing a universal (yet neutral) message that 'excites and engages' your niche of the market.

The tactic then is to generate a compelling home page message that says everything about you except the price, which you will have replaced with your set of brand credentials, including your series of unique features that go way beyond what all the other websites for the same product class can achieve.

Although in terms of pure brand play we know that single-theme focused messages are the best way to promote branded products in any one market, on-line we have to find a universal message that is acceptable to most, if not all. This message must be strong enough to compel people to click into your website once they have looked quickly at your home page, having waited and watched it download.

The opening statements we have employed on LuxuryTies are very neutral in their wording, meeting our market in a friendly way. Some of the opening titles we have previously used are:

Do You Suffer From Bad Tie Days?

The Tie Wearer's Companion

Initially we want to answer a browser's or searcher's immediate question: why are they looking for ties?

The first message delivered on the home page has to be engaging and quick to answer this, bearing in mind we are competing with on- and off-line product counterparts with the same functionality. We must always remember the browser/searcher has a limited attention span and knows that a million other competitors are a click on the 'back' button away.

We regard the home page as a place to say something profound or provocative, as the home page is the start of your presentation. In terms of the average attention span of a browser, your home page has approximately eight seconds to engage them to the point where they actually want to delve further into your website.

The home page has to be short, sharp and snappy, giving over as much easy-to-digest information as possible and ensuring that your name is suddenly interrelated with the generic product term (eg Hunters = ties).

This is what we are currently saying on our home page, and we have found that it successfully engages our visitors:

> ### Tie and shirt matching service with SavileRow.tv film advice from LuxuryTies.com
>
> #### The Tie Wearer's Companion...
>
> Do you suffer from bad tie days wondering why your tie doesn't look as good on you as it does on the model in that style magazine, or do you cringe in fear when faced with having to tie a bow tie?
>
> If you have ever found yourself in these situations then you may now breathe a sigh of relief as help has arrived!
>
> May we be the first to welcome you to our silk tie matching service and SavileRow.tv film productions showing you the 'how tos' of all that is correct in neckwear etiquette by Hunters – Savile Row's Master Silk Tie Maker.

In reading this you will realize that we immediately emphasize the fact that we are the browser's/searcher's friend and are there to help them. We do not talk about low prices or how wonderful our designs are. In fact we avoid all the regular preamble used by the rest of the market, who tend to get straight in with messages about the size of their site, their designs, free delivery and all the other 'junk' that website home pages tend to say.

In fact many of them try to give too much information. Remember – if it's a visual product, show a picture to get your message across and engage the audience, and get your brand into their mindset immediately.

It took us a long time to create the short text message quoted above – reviewing magazines, combining our own research and continually fine-tuning the message as we went along.

The important messages we wanted to express within the body of the text were as follows:

- To tell people what we do.

- To endorse our credentials immediately by saying where we are in the world – London's Savile Row district.

- To answer the question why or give the reason that they (a browser or searcher) are looking for ties or even ask a question with which your audience can identify.

- To employ some limited humour. Do not patronize, and keep to the mindset of the market – it's all about ties, nothing else.

- To be their friend – tell people we are there for them.

- To give people an idea of what they can do in our website that cannot be achieved by visiting a competitor's site – for example LuxuryTies' unique technical capabilities.

This all has to be achieved in less than 120 words – our own target – the reason being that, as always, the competition is just a 'back click away'.

LuxuryTies' home page as a window of opportunity

By dissecting LuxuryTies' home page message/content, we will now explain how we came up with our 'opener'.

As mentioned earlier, there are many websites that have paid absolutely no attention to their home page and the brand value-added messages that need to be conveyed in that part of a website. This becomes an opportunity for you in your own product/service market.

If you go back to the analysis of your brand credentials and brand staircase you should (if you have thought about what's important to your market and where you are in relation to your key purchaser/browser drivers) be able to put this information over in a very succinct manner that answers the key questions posed by the browser/searcher and acts as the basis for a relationship of trust between browser and website.

It is essential to divide your opening message into why you are unique and what you are going to do for the browser. In other words justify your business, its uniqueness and your credentials (including experience if available), including where you are located, and state what you actually sell or provide and why you are a better proposition than all the rest.

You then need to encase this in an overall message that reads in a style appropriate to what you offer, ensuring that the text/content is universally acceptable in its neutrality and is engaging.

Tell people what you do

After having welcomed the browser/searcher a key feature of our text is that we use the word 'tie' seven times, and employ a variation of the word in 'bow ties' and a phrase that browsers in a more senior age range would apply in 'neckwear'.

The most popular generic search term on-line for a site such as LuxuryTies is 'ties', with other words or phrases used such as neck ties. Over 15,134 searches were performed for the word 'ties' during June 2001.

After reading the first two lines of our opening text the searcher knows what we do. So many websites omit that basic information on their home page, leaving the browser to try and guess what it is all about, or read on until their patience finally evaporates.

Endorse your uniqueness

Once people read the text they immediately understand that we sell ties from Savile Row, England, and that they can do a few things with the website that look interesting. Overall it takes about eight seconds to read the first two lines which provide a brief overview of Hunters and the LuxuryTies' site technology.

As this page is our 'shop front to the world' we decided to add a shaded silhouette backdrop of our building, having first ensured that it did not impact on the page's download time. (It is in fact virtually obscured by the text and cannot be seen on some lower version browsers.) This image conveys an important message, as people realize without having to look too hard that it's an old building, and we start to bring in some of the elements of traditional off-line bricks and mortar credentials.

Here you should note that we operate from a Grade II listed building in the London W1 area. Those who do not have such an asset could adopt (for example) a well-known landmark that is instantly recognizable worldwide to bring a visual thought-provoking feature to the website – but make sure the landmark is relevant to what you are about!

We then added the silhouette of our tie label which, when clicked on, operates as the entry button taking the browser to the rest of the site – again a gimmick, but a browser, on placing their cursor on our Hunters' brand label is subconsciously reading our brand name.

Create the relationship – answer a question

We want to establish our friendship immediately and make a browser feel welcome, but we also need to address the question of why are they looking for ties in the first place, or even raise the question of whether they are currently doing something wrong. To do this we ask:

> Do you suffer from bad tie days wondering why your tie doesn't look as
> good on you as it does on the model in that style magazine, or do you
> cringe in fear when faced with having to tie a bow tie?

Each word has been carefully selected to engage the browser quickly. As their friend in this area we ask them if they 'suffer from etc … ' and then describe some of the common problems of our market, which have been identified through research.

Research will identify what's important to 80% of your market, even if you only ask ten people. (That's a limited sample, but at least you will begin to get some ideas that you can develop further.) We mention the two main problems of our tie wearing community: the fact that their ties never look very good on them and the fact that most people cannot tie a bow tie. Through this we lock straight into the key subconscious features of the purchase decision as people want their ties to look good on them.

Because we know our market so well we were able to isolate further reasons why people 'just wanting to buy a tie' should visit us, and we then deliver the LuxuryTies' unique proposition.

Delivering the proposition

We deliver the opening site proposition within the following text:

> May we be the first to welcome you to our silk tie matching service and
> SavileRow.tv film productions showing you the 'how tos' of all that is correct
> in neckwear etiquette by Hunters – Savile Row's Master Silk Tie Maker.

Once we have established with the browser/searcher that we can meet their expectations – in some instances this includes giving information away (though, as you will read later, we don't actually part with the most important data) – they enter LuxuryTies.

You will note we avoid any long words (owing to the widespread geographical nature of our market), and for the main justificatory credential we bring in our location: Savile Row, twice (Savile Row is fairly universally known for tailored clothing). This is part of the establishment of the Hunters' brand credentials and value-added proposition.

Here we focus people on what they can achieve in our website that goes beyond what they could do with all the other tie-related websites (remember we use the term 'all that is correct in neckwear etiquette', a very Savile Rowish phrase), including the famous brand sites. In fact we review ten of our on-line competitors in the same product class regularly to ensure that we are more appealing to our target market through our opening statements.

At the very start of the entire browser finding/searching process we don't want to talk about our ties and we don't want to talk about price. We just want to give the browser enough information to whet their appetite so that they click on the Hunters' tie label 'enter' button to view and use the site's technology features, while quietly gaining experience with the Hunters' brand.

Understanding your brand's location in its market

During our graduate research in 1997, a feature we identified in developing a brand is that it has to be seen among the leaders in the same product class to derive credibility 'by association'.

As mentioned earlier, if you view the shelves in a department store you will see a number of similar products by famous brands across a range of prices, and somewhere on that shelf you will see the store's own-brand, displayed in just the same way as the main brands but normally at a lower price. The idea behind this is that we as consumers will regard the store's own brand as every bit as good as the main brands and will even regard it as an acceptable alternative to these big names.

We regard website positioning as pretty much the same when using the techniques of optimization since you are aiming for your website to be seen among the big names so that your product/service will be regarded as 'the suitable alternative'.

But with the internet creating such wide markets for the same basic product or service offering, we know we are better off focusing our marketing efforts towards a niche or segment of the total market. We can service a niche best for the reasons mentioned earlier, where uniqueness and differentiation are the keys to a customer's decision-making process.

It is still every bit as important to be returned in the top results for a generic search and to be seen alongside the household brand names, but we have to ensure that we meet the more specialized interest market grouping.

We discussed the role of the search engines in marketing earlier, but it's worth mentioning at this stage that there is no better feeling than seeing your website in a number one position for an overall generic term category – the category killer. At the time of writing, we are number five on AOL for the search term 'neckties' and number six on Netscape for the search term 'ties'.

Previously we have occupied generic term pole position (number one) across many engines, and we continually move up and down the starting grid position (or leader board) for our product category. But that's the web – the positions are never fixed, they have to be continually worked on.

High generic term positions are valuable to us, making LuxuryTies visible to the monthly 15,000 or so tie searchers, and they have taken us approximately a year to achieve.

Alongside the Hunters' LuxuryTies website in the search engine's results set returned, you will find many of the other famous clothing brands. But it is our website's uniqueness that wins us the visitors and, ultimately, the market's take-up of our offering, not the fact that we pour millions into advertising (which we don't).

But our brand's proposition is different from the major names. We reach out to just a small segment of the total daily tie-wearing market of 600 million – in cyberspace our location is that of a niche supplier and our segment offering is tuned to the Savile Row interest group whose tastes are for classical, timeless styling and elegance.

To find out what our market actually looks like we analyzed the different buyer groups that made up this total tie-wearing market and assessed how, when we found them, we could optimize towards any particular segment of the tie market and engage our target browser group in their own terms.

From Figure 9.1 you will see that Hunters' market is segmented between a variety of tie wearers and buyer groups. All have a need for ties, understand our product and are already educated in most aspects of neckties. All we want to do is build on that through the credentials of our brand and our website's unique capabilities to assist them in a more refined way of selecting ties from Savile Row, something many had never done before.

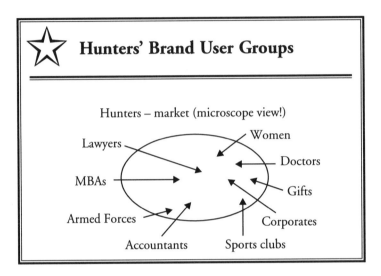

Figure 9.1 The segmented tie market.

It is important to be able to visualize your market in this way as it helps focus your business towards your customers and their real needs. In our own studies we found that virtually all markets are comprised of a number of smaller markets that go to create the overall market.

When we look back at the funded e-businesses who land-grabbed, many never altered their customer proposition to meet the smaller segments. This is yet another reason why they failed so quickly as they attempted to engage the total market. (By now, as an unknown brand operating within highly competitive global economic and emerging information-driven cultures, you should realize that this is virtually impossible.)

We realize that consumers have subconscious codes that we have to tap into and adapt to across cultures and economies. With this in mind and drawing on your product's credentials/unique offering, you should be able to understand why the message has to be personalized (the fine-tuning), as what is important to one user group pales into insignificance with others. At the same time, any message you employ has to be neutral in the first instance to ensure people will read on, their imagination captured.

As an example, suppose Hunters wished to focus on the market segment defined as 'sports clubs', who purchase ties of a single design for their members. The requirement of the buyer group becomes a design theme comprising sporting motifs, volume and price. For comparison, the requirement for legal groups is quality and Savile Row authenticity. In this case the deciding feature becomes a traditional and conservative look in keeping with their occupation.

As we examined the segments further we went on to discover that each segment is multilayered, with each layer building on (or increasing the user's expectations of) the last. We therefore develop our messages further still as we hone in on each layer's individuality and its own unique needs, in our attempt to engage them.

Again, careful research of your market is what really pays dividends. Most new websites were set up to meet whole markets, which were defined in terms of numbers of users.

What the new media e-businesses failed to address was that the markets comprise customers who are individuals, with different expectations as to what the product/brand can do for them and, most importantly, what it could mean to them.

In adopting this strategy the mega-funded dotcom businesses failed to tune into their market and thus wasted vast sums attempting to open/create markets that may well have existed, had they spoken to their market on a more personal segment-by-segment then layer-by-layer basis. They would then have had a chance to grow their businesses slowly rather than crashing and burning so quickly.

To 'speak' to the different groups we have to alter or rearrange our brand's personality factors through our home page message and focus our on-line promotion activities to the niche/segment selected.

You should by now start to envisage how your brand will speak to your niche, putting itself across as a friend as you offer a value-added, unique proposition that goes beyond the mass marketing websites. The best businesses (and the most profitable) are those that have highly differentiated sector-specific product offerings that are (as stated) only available from a limited number of outlets – in our case LuxuryTies with its special range of Hunters' brand tie designs, by means of a unique technology experience which helps the tie wearer exercise their choice.

Really the fundamental premise is that LuxuryTies does not *sell* ties – it helps people to choose ties and increases their information and knowledge of them through the Hunters' Savile Row brand – where better to learn from? And in helping with the choice there's a strong possibility that we might just win an order.

Gathering intelligence on your target segment

We always base any segment selection around the following considerations:

- How big is the niche or segment?

- Can we grow it?

- Who else is operating in it or is it new?

- Are they entrenched competition? How long have they been there?

- Could we add to it in terms of delivering something new and innovative?

- How fast can we engage it?

- Would we need anything new in terms of assets to meet it?

The idea behind our questions relate to the fact that we do not want to enter a small narrow segment where we have to compete head-on with another niche player. This will involve cost and the time needed to secure a foothold in the market will be longer.

Also we strongly believe that it is better to be at the front of your own niche, cashing in on the secondary or splinter market that has been created through the marketing and advertising expenditure of the bigger funded websites who have induced the browser to make a generic search of the total market in the first place. There will always be a segment of any market that wants something a bit different – a more unique offering, style or choice.

Most business people would refer to this as the 80/20 rule: 80% of the market fits the standard model and 20% falls outside. More often than not it is the 20% of the total market that is the most profitable, it just needs to be serviced differently and this is something that only niche players can do (the specialist versus generalist rule).

For the smaller on-line business this presents a fantastic opportunity. The 'land-grab' theorists would attack the total market, and in doing so ignore the difference between user segments/layers that actually make up the total market for the product.

One of the best and easiest places to collect market intelligence, including in what way and where the big companies (mostly your competitors) are going to make their next play, is to watch their websites continually, join their mailing lists for newsletters and keep trying to think like a member of their management team.

Imagine that you have the same funding as your nearest competitor; knowing your product or service sector as well as you do, you will find that your options are just as limited as they were before you received your imaginary funding. As you get to know your competitor better you will start to see the pitfalls of their strategies and how you can benefit by being a smaller focused niche company with the added advantage that you can manoeuvre faster.

You will be surprised at how quickly you can gather intelligence on your competitors through the financial sites on the internet. When you sit down and read through all the data you have collected the chances are you'll know more about the direction they are heading in than their own CEO!

For example, we once came across an on-line company (in the same sector as Hunters) whose press release gave a great insight into the giftware market for ties. It had been posted on a website carrying public information before the organization had actually geared itself up to do anything about 'the new market'. We think the reason for this was to give their shareholders' morale a boost by laying claim to future profitable revenue streams, despite the massive losses being built up behind them.

However, the release gave us the opportunity to monitor the styles and designs they later presented to the market for a three-month period while they warmed up potential customers through their saturation advertising.

We, meanwhile, sat in the background viewing and evaluating their pricing strategies and other factors necessary to engage the market. We were then able to define LuxuryTies' role in winning a chunk of the market – but only after this company had started the ball rolling.

If you consider that according to the 80/20 rule it is the last 20% of the overall market that is going to pick up the advertising tab for the whole exercise and ensure the profits of the total activity, then we must have made a small dent in that at no cost to our business. All it took was some recalibration of our home page and its programming to respond to the generic searches a browser would be using who had seen the advertising on the search engine with which this competitor had a partnership, but without using their name or any of their words, terms or phrases.

Really this is what a small internet business is all about. We stated earlier that competition is fierce – we just have to employ the same tactics as the others to generate and win new business. We have even been subject to exactly the same 'roll-over' by competitors.

We have always regarded business (on- or off-line) as a game of cat and mouse, and we are continually being forced to think up new ways to engage the market through the unique value-added process. Who says business life isn't exciting!

Incidentally, on one particular search engine when we type in the term 'Hunters ties' we are currently first, followed by about 118,000 other websites that have employed that term in their optimization – all leading to gambling and adult-content websites. The good thing about this is that Hunters achieve more brand/product name exposure – and it is related to ties as all the sites returned have the phrase in their description tag 'Hunters ties'.

We are all competing for the same consumers' disposable income/browser time. It is how we win that from other organizations that makes the difference. This 'rip off' being used by these other websites gives us a bit of generic brand ability as it's the association between the words 'Hunters' and 'ties' creating a brand for Hunters as a tie maker that helps us out, even if we are being 'rolled' and our browsers' attentions are redirected elsewhere.

Selecting the target browser/search group

Hunters (like you by now) are different from the rest of the same website marketing pack as we are a niche speciality brand.

We know we have to alter our home page (only the home page and its programming in the first instance) towards the many different user groups at any one time, depending on which tie designs (or product) we are offering to meet an identified niche. We then resubmit the home page (only) to the appropriate categories of search engines and directories.

For example, if we are running a range of regimental stripe designs (eg British Army stripes) we have to focus our home page towards those who are interested in the British Army and its traditions in order to engage this specialized interest group. Alternatively, if we are running a range of endangered species animal tie designs (eg pandas) we have to refocus the language on our site to reach out to the type of buyer group interested in such issues.

For us the product offering is the tie design. This should be replaced by the information or product/service you supply, supported by your unique added value to underpin why people should enter your site once they have found you in – of course – the highest ranking position for your product class.

The importance of this tactic in a brand development framework is highly relevant, as a brand meets the lifestyle or aspirational needs of a selected group. So if you become known for a highly relevant product/service, there is a good chance that your e-business will become regarded as the brand for that offering.

Over time you will be able to develop new products/services to increase your portfolio of offerings while retaining the original product foundation that was the source of competitive advantage for your organization in the first place. (For example, Hunters continues to sell traditional tie designs on-line, but has increased its product portfolio to include cufflinks, scarves and other related accessories.)

We strongly believe that you should never dispense with what people originally liked about you. Just add to it while relating your additions back to your original foundations.

Going back to Figure 9.1, let's say we decide to select a new market segment to optimize LuxuryTies towards. The target group is that of MBAs (the academic business qualification Master of Business Administration), as a valuable tie wearing community and potential market for the Hunters' brand via LuxuryTies. Assume at this stage that our choice is based on the fact that we have some experience or prior knowledge of this market.

We first have to conduct some live field research using the internet to give us an overall feel for the market. We can then answer the standard segment selection questions detailed earlier:

• Who is the market?

• Where could we fit in?

• Why should they want our offering?

We can then start to rate the segments and eventually select the one in which we can move most quickly.

With the above in mind, our own one-hour on-line research on MBA-focused and other related websites gave us the following intelligence:

• There are 2 million MBA graduates in the world.

• 90,000 new MBAs graduate each year.

- MBA graduates are globally dispersed in high-profile management positions.

- Earnings are in the high income range.

- There are strong alumni associations (university associations).

- There is a well-supported on-line MBA community using the internet for research, finding new vacancies, etc.

- There is not an MBA-specific graduation/gift tie that we could find on/off-line.

- There is a high proportion of male MBAs (important as it is mostly men who wear ties).

The value of this information to you as a niche brand website marketer who is opting for a segment-specific concentration strategy are:

- You know what the market is.

- You know how you are going to engage it.

- You know its current and future predicted size.

- You can apply some quantitative analysis (sales volumes).

- You know the market opportunity – there is no current producer of specific graduation and gift ties to this market.

- You know that the vast majority of MBAs reside in the US – this has an impact on the kind of home page language you will employ.

To us at Hunters this market certainly looks attractive, and that's just after a one-hour on-line research session. In fact the most important research data has been summarized in about two short paragraphs and therefore we know as much about the target market as anyone else does. (Many old-school CEOs will have paid an external marketing consultant to perform such research for them thinking that was the right thing to do. Let's face it, what better way to justify your existence than to stalk around the office with a glossy report under your arm, because that always makes someone look important?)

As a segment for comparison (as one option is no option) let's take another group, say the Armed Forces, where our on-line (again one-hour) research found the following:

- They are globally dispersed – we could not find any data as to on-line usage by service personnel or websites that they most visit.

- There are a large number of regiments – about 500 in the UK.

- There is strong off-line purchasing ability through stores and barracks.

- The market is highly competitive on-line – price factors also come into play as it's a saturated market.

- There are alternative buyer groups – those who were members of the forces and those who were not. This means that two different messages would have to be created in terms of depth of product/regiment knowledge to engage the buyer group doing the purchasing.

Clearly this is a case of a very localized and narrow niche, and the product offering itself doesn't have the newness of appeal that an on-line product/service needs to bring in website visitors.

It is important to note that many of the start-up businesses went ahead with very localized products/services that had no value or market outside their own countries. This is really how, where and why the VC money was blown.

No organization can say that the UK browser base will make up the mainstay of its business activity on-line. The management must possess international experience, which many of the ex-corporate CEOs didn't have. Primarily they were too blinkered in their outlook – coming from a big UK company doesn't mean you are going to create a big UK on-line company when the audience is international.

However, the regimental tie market is not that attractive to us. It is too wide as a market in terms of product range, with a large number of regiments whose ties we would have to offer the market. In fact we don't even know – and still we cannot find out – which is the top selling regimental tie. However, the fact that two different messages are needed will confuse one half of the market. For example, an ex-service person will buy a regimental tie because they were in the forces; alternatively someone will buy a regimental tie because they like the colours. Is it a fashion item or a historic/functional item, or is it both?

We could engage the market on the basis that the designs are traditional and authentic for those who like the history of the British Army, but some form of superior back-up information would need to be provided if we were to go into this market at a better level than all the existing market suppliers.

Therefore the total content/information requirement is high. As we have identified a number of established players already operating with good search engine positions for regimental ties and even greater off-line store locations, the chances of making an on-line success of this market are low.

We realize that we could easily compete through price, but time is also a factor (in business it always is). We want segments where we move in and out quickly – even though we are in the total market for the long term with our Hunters' brand we continually jump from one segment to another. We always regard our movement in the market as an important part of the Hunters' brand. The premise is that as if you stay in one place for too long with exactly the same product offering (in our case tie designs) you will lose your competitive edge, and run the risk of becoming typecast.

To some people Hunters is known for club ties, to others for conservative ties and to some for regimental ties (we do actually sell a few). What we try to ensure is that the foundation brand – 'Hunters equals ties' – is reinforced regularly to keep us fresh and in the market's thoughts.

When you are creating or carving out a new niche in an existing market, everyone wants to take a look at what you are offering. But markets do have a tendency to mature very quickly for single-product companies and there are always new entrants undercutting you and increasing the value-added proposition beyond what you can provide. Remember innovation in technology can never be regarded as the ultimate source of long-term advantage.

A number of businesses were first into the market but only a few have ever been able to retain their edge. In many instances the first entrant is beaten by other organizations entering the market later with a greater physical or critical mass and using their financial muscle to swallow up markets overnight, thus winning complete control.

Your business may be in such a situation – the first with a new innovation but finding it difficult to build on it. In this sort of situation it is going to be a difficult and long campaign as you witness your sales decline and eventually your choices are reduced to leaving the market in search of new pastures or closing the business completely.

In our experience as a small business operating on-line (and possibly off-line) the two best times to join a market are:

- at the beginning, if you have created it, to pick up the 'we want to be the first' customer

- as the market matures, to pick up the 'I'd like something just a bit different' customer.

What happens in between is that the market becomes bogged down by competitor businesses all chasing the same reducing customer base with fundamentally the same product that's undergone a few adaptations here and there along the way. People as consumers will normally tend towards the lowest price supplier in such a mass market situation.

CHAPTER 10

Creating the market niche

Entering and developing a market through e-commerce can be a fairly low-cost proposition, providing that segment of your market actually goes on-line to look for what you are offering.

Often it's a case of recalibrating your home page if you have an existing website or generating one (if you are new to this) and then making your move through focused search engine/directory market optimization to secure the key phrases and search terms that browsers/searchers use.

Some websites (mainly the off-the-shelf packages) tend not to have a home page that can be optimized and you may have to (if you own and operate such a site) buy space on a server to host your new page that redirects or links to your main website.

You must make sure you have a page available for optimization on your website and it is best if it is the home page. With LuxuryTies we only ever fully optimize the home page, not the entire site, basically as it is more efficient in terms of time.

LuxuryTies has a home page high in the search engine rankings with the generic terms particular to its product class – 'ties' and 'neck ties' – across a range of the top twenty engines. This is the starting position for us as we can then reach out to other segments of the tie market using the generic search term 'ties' as the foundation, eg 'MBA ties', or 'ties MBA'.

For example, if we go back to our shoelace browser route map in Figure 8.2, we might have a search engine position number nine for the generic term

---

'shoelaces', but as we have now added 'multi-coloured shoelaces' to our product range to meet an identified segment that wants a more unique offering, we have to alter the optimization towards the needs of our new profile markets. However, we still want to be in the top ten for our generic search terms.

We want to include our new multi-coloured shoelaces in our site description (the few short lines that appear on the search engine/directory result page) where you describe what you are offering. Suddenly we can reach this new segment of the market – possibly the top 20% or the premium end of the market.

Our objective in this exercise is to achieve a high ranking in the first instance for a generic term (shoelaces), and then exploit that with other product/service offerings that we have (our additional value added) ie, shoelaces (the generic) followed by multi-coloured shoelaces (our unique product extension).

We must maintain the high search engine position for the generic product term to be able to perform this exercise and as we have said, generic terms/phrases are continually fought over in the world of e-commerce. To us and our competitors a high ranking position for the term 'ties' is worth its weight in gold providing it is on one of the top engines and the term is frequently used to conduct a search.

To engage our new market segment we have to make the following changes to our home page:

- We have to alter our description tag.

- We have to bring forward some of the keywords in our string of words contained within our optimized home page programming.

- We have to ensure the home page text/content speaks to the browser/searcher in line with their mindset and is fine-tuned to their subconscious codes.

Segment selection criteria

For Hunters the choice becomes very simple in our exercise to select a new segment as we look at the two identified segments of the market side by side, in our case MBAs versus regimental tie-wearers.

The MBA market is one where we can quantify size and possible value, and we know pretty much how to reach out to it as, although the market is new to us, it is based on ties. The regimental tie market on the other hand is mature, and we can't add much to it in terms of product offering – in reality it has become driven by price. Matters are compounded by the fact that it is the regiment that decides which colours go in to make up their design (in many instances there are reasons why odd colours are employed) and we cannot alter the tie design. We also face massive problems in having to explain these facts to some cultures, who regard regimental ties simply as attractively striped tie designs in bold colours but want to know a bit more about them before they buy.

Having decided on the MBA market, to reach and engage this new market we have to ensure we remain high for the generic term 'ties' and then add additional optimization to our home page. In the message we put over in the content/text we include new terms and generic phrases such as 'MBA Graduation Gifts', 'Gifts for MBAs', 'MBAs', etc. mixing the initials 'MBA' with our other product generic terms/words. Our location in cyberspace then alters from a 'general appeal tie website' to one focused on and targeting the MBA tie-wearing niche of the overall market. We consider that (at best) this will have a lifetime of, say, six months.

The steps we would take to meet this market are summarized as follows:

- Design a range of MBA graduation ties (you might change the information you are currently presenting to meet the specific niche), giving something unique to our visitors/browsers in terms of a product they can't get anywhere else.

- Re-optimize our home page towards the search engine/directory we are targeting. This may include changes to the background programming: keywords, title tag, meta description (all explained fully in Part 4).

- Submit our new home page to the search engines and directories.

- Review our rankings and re-optimize to meet any shortfalls in position, normally six to eight weeks after the first-round submissions. In some instances it can take up to three months to see the benefit of your work on some search engines/directories.

In constructing the new home page content we would draw in features of how our uniqueness has been realigned to this MBA market segment, and establish in a few short words why MBAs (or those looking for gifts for graduating MBAs) should take a look at what we have designed.

We would ensure that our site's home page programming is itself capable of responding to searches where the term 'MBA' is being employed by a browser. We will cover this in the technical chapters of Part 4, but Figure 10.1 gives an insight into the browser route map for looking at LuxuryTies' range of Hunters' MBA ties.

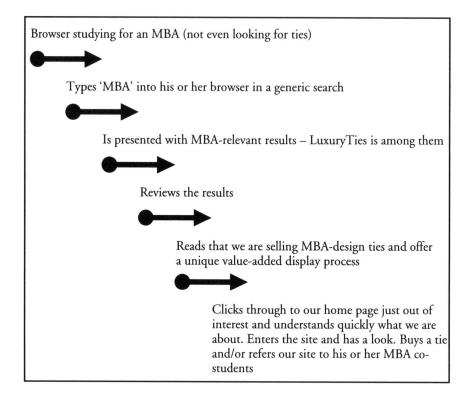

Figure 10.1 Map outlining browser search pattern.

This might seem impossible, but the internet does have a habit of redirecting people's attention from their original search. (Some say it takes an average of five visits before a browser converts into a sale. We have no experience of this average – it is just another internet statistic that we have come across on our travels and have no way of verifying. However, it's interesting all the same to think someone actually worked it out!)

Today there exists the concept of 'viral marketing' where people refer our site on to others who would be interested in looking at, say, our MBA ties, who then refer it on to others etc etc. Through this the chances of our getting a 'name' for MBA ties is increased, as are the prospects of selling them providing there is something unique about them and the market is ready.

LuxuryTies generates orders from all over the world, but we are always surprised when we receive orders from countries where we didn't think ties in our price range would have a market. Viral marketing cannot be underestimated as the 'word of mouse' is a strong influencer, providing you are offering something novel in an imaginative way that is only available from a single or limited number of outlets/channels or the originating source. Other people will pass your details on, and a chain occurs.

Using your unique value-added proposition to collect browser data

During our research we focused on a funded men's accessory-related site, who during their first year had achieved 12,000 customer registrations, whereas during LuxuryTies' first year (on a £500 promotion budget) 2,000 registrations were achieved or 16% of that level.

Earlier on in this text we described capturing customer information through operating a unique value-added service. We explain here (briefly) how we managed that through LuxuryTies and just how it can be achieved in a low-cost and simple way. (A full e-CRM [Customer Relationship Management] tactic is outside the scope of this text.)

If you are (like us) a small company, apart from sales themselves, perhaps the most important information you can gain on-line are the names and e-mail addresses of those who have visited your website, as they have shown a specific interest in what you do and may turn out to be customers in the future.

Once you have been able to undertake the steps explained in this book, you should think seriously about protecting your value-added customer proposition by designing a means of collecting browser/site visitor information. We achieved this by adding a simple registration page to our website that saves the browser's basic data, the idea being that before someone gets to view the unique element of the website they part with some information as a form of trade off.

If you know who has looked at your website, and you have a means of collecting this information (which doesn't infringe the data protection legislation), you are on your way to creating a customer database. Such databases are extremely valuable and larger organizations will take competitors over (consolidate them) on the strength of a high level of customer registrations as a faster means of accessing new markets – or, as is normally the case, when their own marketing teams have run out of ideas to generate new customers.

The way we managed to achieve this and create a useable customer database was to think about the biggest element of LuxuryTies that added value in a novel way. Was a visitor receiving value in being able to mix and match shirts and ties? Or perhaps it was watching the videos where we show people how to tie bow ties – another on-line source of competitive advantage for LuxuryTies that adds to our unique in-depth product proposition.

As we sat and discussed this issue with a London software design company, they pointed out that we could get browsers/viewers to register their details before they were given access to the film clips as it was this single area that provided the greatest value to a browser – a unique insight into Savile Row's Master Silk Tie Makers showing how to tie the perfect Windsor knot, how to repair frayed ties and why stripe directions vary.

This answered our question about how to gain some information to our future advantage. We could use this later in an e-mail newsletter to update past site visitors about alterations to our on-line designs etc, say from traditional designs to themes of endangered species and so on.

To us the real intellectual property in LuxuryTies lies in the customer information; for the customer it is learning from Savile Row – and thus a fair trade arises. However, while many people rightly state that intellectual property and intellectual capital can be protected through trademarks and registrations, we have found this to be a very expensive project, especially in our case as we would have to try and register the whole process worldwide (or in as many of those countries where viable registration is possible).

Summary

We have covered a lot in this section. As is always the case, the only way to understand many of the techniques and concepts is to employ them yourself.

By now you will have learned: the importance of selecting segments; setting messages for your segment of the total market; how, by adding a new home page message/programming to meet a level of the segment, you can engage browsers/customers in a very low-cost and friendly manner.

Research is always the key to any promotion strategy. It is vitally important that you know your market, and can relate to it through your brand. The internet makes it easier than ever to gather and collate market data and intelligence. This alone can reduce the inherent risks when entering and trying to develop new markets.

These days you can reach new markets for your products/services through optimizing your home page to tackle a segment. If that doesn't work you can try and find another segment and repeat the exercise. In the days before the internet it would have been a massive marketing exercise of immense cost to evaluate and 'contact' the market in terms of advertising.

In Part 4 we will take you through the technical aspects of the entire process. If you take time to study these chapters and visualize where the process could and should be used by your organization, we believe you will find success.

PART 4

Techniques used in website optimization

Note. Before you embark on the following chapters we recommend you study the examples of HTML (hyper text mark-up language) and the glossary of optimization terms provided in Appendices A and B at the end of the book.

CHAPTER 11

Why use search engines?

The internet is perhaps one of the last decade's most controversial business and social topics, paving the way to some of the most intense 'get rich quick schemes' – and in some cases scams – overnight.

Chain letters that were originally sent through traditional mail are now being delivered in their hundreds of thousands via e-mail globally, spawning the growth of MLM (multi-level marketing) firms with the promise of immediate financial success for little or no effort on your part!

With all the controversy that has arisen and all of the bad feedback we have heard and continue to hear – the most recent at the time of writing being Excite.UK closing its doors – many businesses have chosen not to venture into the world of internet marketing, a decision that has actually hindered the success of their overall business.

The fact is that a small business can develop a high-profile presence on the internet and become very successful with a minimium of investment. As with any company, you need to promote or advertise it along with the products or services you sell or offer to as wide an audience as possible (the market) that's focused towards your offering.

Technically, a website is just another form of advertising media. However, in order for people to find and see this advertisement, it must be visible. Thus our main focus in this part will be the methods of on-line promotion we use to attract potential clients to our website via the use of search engines.

Here we will introduce you to the tools and knowledge that will take your e-business to its next technical level, giving you the ability to enter the vast world of e-commerce with the confidence that you will be successful and your investment will not be wasted.

Throughout this part, we will provide worked examples and useful website addresses for your convenience. Most software and resources mentioned in this section can be found at our website http://www.websurfer-netcafe.com.

In order for you to take full advantage of this material and achieve the greatest results you should:

- have a general understanding of HTML (hyper text mark-up language), the programming language used to design web pages

- be comfortable with the hierarchy of files and directories and possess a general understanding of Microsoft Windows-based software applications, eg Adobe, Word, Windows, etc.

We will also discuss the merits of various types of software used for tracking, promoting and optimizing your website, including the design and hosting services, to help you enhance your e-business online. Upon completion of this part, you will possess a general understanding of website promotional methods using search engines, and be able to attract the focused website visitor traffic your business needs.

As mentioned earlier, it is estimated that over 80% of all visitor traffic to a website is derived from the major search engines/directories and of all the different methods used to find a website these are the number one resource, even more so than opt-in e-mail lists and banner advertising.

Let's take a quick look at banner ads in a little more depth and how they are designed to work. You pay a substantial fee to have a company place your banner on their website to be displayed to their visitors.

The first question you have to ask is how relevant to what you are doing is the website that is displaying your banner advertisement? By that we mean is the traffic (ie the visitors to the website) looking for what you have to sell or offer on the website hosting your banner ad. As an example, suppose you wanted to buy airline tickets and were at an airline website, would you suddenly switch your attention to a banner advertising cookware? What are the chances that others will click on it? What's the relevance?

Junk e-mail is just the same. About 99.999% of what we all receive isn't relevant to us, and as it has such a high cost in organizing, distributing etc we question the validity of such a method to drive focused, eager customers to a website – unless something is being offered for free, and, let's face it, there's nothing free in this world!

With this in mind, wouldn't it make sense for the search engines to be your primary focus when promoting your company's website rather than paying for opt-in e-mails or banner advertising? Considering the statistics for results and the cost involved, search engines give you 'the biggest bang for your buck' when it comes to promoting and advertising your website to a specific audience.

Search engines take all the guesswork out of the problem. When a visitor comes to your website from a search engine they have already made a conscious decision that they want or need your product or service. Your purchase to visitor ratio will be substantially higher with visitors who arrive through a search engine against those who arrive from banner ads, opt-in e-mail etc. Also bear in mind that if your ratio is much higher (search engine visitors versus opt-ins), you won't need as much traffic to make the same amount of sales.

Banners ads and opt-in e-mail lists are methods that generally focus on quantity, not quality. For instance, let's say that a website you have paid to display your banner gets 1,000 hits a day and 1% of those visitors actually click on your banner and visit your site. We will also assume that you have the most attractive website on the internet and that 50% of your visitors purchase something from you. This would equate to about five sales a day, not bad depending on what you are actually selling.

Now let's say you get 100 visitors a day from the search engines directly to your site. Bearing in mind that these visitors are looking for your product or services already and assuming that you only get 10% to make a purchase, that would equate to 10 sales per day on just a tenth of the traffic. Just think – what if you were to get a 50% purchase rate or you were to get 500 or 1,000 visitors a day? What would your sales be like then?

As with anything worthwhile (or profitable) you must be dedicated to achieving the results that you need in order to be successful. It will take hard work and patience to gain the highest results – if you only put in a little time and effort, you can't expect to generate fabulous results.

Of course, what your website covers will also determine how competitive your market is. The more competitive the market the more difficult it will be to achieve and maintain high placement in the search engines for a long period of time.

Let's do a little experiment. Go to http://www.altavista.com and do a search on the key phrase 'search engine ranking' without using the quotes. How many search results did it return?

You will see that there are millions of results for this three-word phrase. In order for a prospective client to find your website through the use of search engines, you must aim to be within the top 30–40 results when the market is highly competitive or on the first or second page. If you are not, the chances are you will not win enough traffic for your site to be successful.

There is a crazy myth circulating that you can simply purchase some form of search engine submission software, submit your website(s) to thousands of search engines, link lists, on-line classifieds, etc and have more traffic than your website's server can handle. Well, let's look at some statistics:

- First – and once again just to get the message home – it is estimated that 85–95% of all traffic to a website is derived from the top 20 search engines: Google, Yahoo, MSN Search, AltaVista, Excite, Ask Jeeves, GoTo, Netscape, Hotbot, Inktomi, Looksmart, Lycos, Go, NBCi, Fast (all the web), ODP (open source directory), AOL Search, Northern Light, Webcrawler, Direct Hit. So why waste your time submitting to thousands of search engines when 20 provide the most traffic? The amount of work needed for an extra 10–15% more traffic is an inefficient use of time.

- Second, surveys have determined that the average internet user will only look through the first 30–40 results or the first and second page of results returned following a search.

- Third, many search engines are actually starting to ignore automated search engine submissions in an attempt to help reduce spam.

However, let's assume you ignore these facts and go ahead and purchase some search engine submission software that automatically submits your site to thousands of search engines – then reality hits. You get nowhere near the amount of traffic promised because your site does not get listed for whatever reason or is listed so far down in the rankings that no one will ever find it.

The lesson here is that you must be listed as close to the top of the results returned as possible. The closer you are to the top, the more traffic you will win and the more sales your website will make.

The remainder of this part will focus on methods and techniques available for achieving top listings within the engines and directories, plus examples of their use and where to employ the techniques to best advantage.

CHAPTER 12

Keywords, keyword relevancy and keyword density

Keywords and key phrases are to a website's positioning on a search engine as a foundation is to a solid building, and without understanding how keywords work, you are not likely to achieve much success in obtaining a proper search engine placement for your website.

Keywords/key phrases are what your potential clients will search under when they go to a search engine. For instance, if you were looking for a computer printer, you would go to a search engine and in the search field you would type 'printers'.

Now, just using the single word 'printer' would return millions of results as there are so many ways in which the word can be used including publishers, printing equipment, computer printers, etc. In order to get a more accurate search, you would need to make a two or more word phrase that describes what you are looking for. Let's say that you are looking for a 'Hewlett Packard printer' – searching on this key phrase leaves no doubt as to what you want.

The volume of results returned will be significantly less, but far more accurate and closer to what you are actually looking for. Due to the sheer volume of websites on the internet today, users have come to realize that they have to search using multiple words or key phrases in order to filter out the amount of results returned and find what they are looking for in a more efficient and relevant manner.

Realistically, with the technological advancements and all the time-saving gadgets available in today's society, people do not have the patience to sort through reams of information and will not hesitate to go elsewhere to get what they want if there is a possibility of getting it faster.

Relevancy of the keywords that you choose to target also comes into play with regard to obtaining a top search engine listing. When we talk about *relevancy* we are referring to the accuracy of your keywords to describe your product or service. Just as a prospective customer will use multiple words/phrases to find what they are looking for when they use a search engine, you must determine what phrases you want to target when deciding to implement optimization strategies and techniques.

One of the first tasks you must address is to create a series of keywords and key phrases that you want to target. There are several methods you can use to determine which keywords/key phrases are pertinent to your customers/business. For instance, you can subscribe to a service that will e-mail you regular reports about the most popular words and phrases used in searches (you can find a link at http://www.websurfer-netcafe.com).

However, it is wise to establish a list of the closest, most important keywords/key phrases that you *yourself* would search on to find your product or service and focus on these first. They are the ones that you will use to optimize your home page/index.html (htm) (the page that will be viewed when someone enters your domain name, http://www.websurfer-netcafe.com for example).

Key word frequency is another term that you need to be aware of – during your research and in the course of this book you will have come across this term regularly. We define this as the number of times that a specific keyword is used throughout a web page regardless of its position. For instance, if we are targeting 'printers' and our web page has exactly 100 words, if the word 'printers' is used three times on that page there would be a keyword frequency of 3% (3 divided by 100) for the word 'printers'.

Depending on the search engine that you are specifically optimizing to (remembering that each search engine and directory should be regarded as a separate market with its own indexing protocols etc) the keyword frequency needed in order to achieve a top ranking can vary from 0.05% to as high as 8% (or more) in relation to your total text count.

Part of the work that is involved with search engine optimizing is experimenting to determine what works and what doesn't. Automating your tasks in order to get more done will have a major impact on how much time you will have to spend on optimizing your website.

GRSoftware has produced a tremendous little programme called KDA (Keyword Density Analyzer). (You will find links to learn more about KDA at our website http://www.websurfer-netcafe.com.) We use the GRKda software for assistance in analyzing websites to determine the correct keyword density.

Another term that you will hear quite often is *keyword prominence*. This term is used to describe how close to the start of the area a keyword appears, for example:

• If a keyword appears at the beginning of an area (or text), its prominence will be 100%.

• If a keyword appears in the middle of an area (or text), its prominence will be around 50%.

• If the keyword appears at the beginning of the area (or text), and another repetition appears at the end of the area, the prominence would be 50%.

• If the keyword appears at the end of the area (or text), prominence would be 0%.

We will provide more examples of key word prominence as we progress through the following chapters.

CHAPTER 13

HTML tags

HTML (hyper text mark-up language) is the programming language used to design a website. You can find further resources regarding HTML at http://www.amazon.com.

In this chapter we will cover the different HTML tags that are important in order to accomplish a top listing in the major search engines (see also the HTML illustration provided in Appendix A). When a search engine spiders your web page it indexes the text between the different HTML tags that we will be discussing in this chapter.

HTML <title></title> tag

The first and arguably the most important HTML tag that we need to review is the <title></title> tag. The content (text) that you place in the HTML title (between the > </) tag will appear in the very top of your browser. It is also the first tag when you view a web page's source code.

To view a web page's source code or HTML try the following:

- In Internet Explorer right click the mouse button on a website's home page (non-flash ones normally work better) then click the View Source command. This will open up a window (usually in Notepad) and will display the HTML source code for the web page you are currently viewing.

- Alternatively for Netscape users click on View in the tool bar and then click on Page Source. That will open up a window (usually in Notepad) that will display the HTML source code for the web page that you are viewing.

Go to http://www.websurfer-netcafe.com and follow the above instructions on how to view the source code. Note the first few lines of code, which should look like this:

```
<html>
<head>
<title>Websurfer Netcafe website positioning
promotion ranking techniques tips tricks and how
to's</title>
<meta name="description" content="Websurfer Netcafe, your
marketing resource location for website
promotion">
<meta name="keywords" content="websurfer netcafe website
promotion positioning placement website search
engine positioning positioning optimization
ranking resource services training techniques
marketing free advertising analysis consulting">
</head>
```

Paying close attention to the content between the **bold <title></title>** tags (set in a mono-spaced font), return to your browser and note what appears in the very top left corner of your browser's title bar. This is also the text that a search engine will index when spidering your website.

This is *the* most important HTML tag. Most of the top search engines place the highest level of importance on this HTML tag. If the search engines' own technology places this kind of importance on this specific tag, it is safe to assume that you should as well.

As a rule of thumb, you should place your keywords at the beginning of the title tag. However, there is always an exception to the rule. To be sure of the proper placement of your keywords, you should subscribe to some form of reporting service like 'The Unfair Advantage Book on Winning the Search Engine Wars' – there is a link on our site http://www.websurfer-netcafe.com.

The report provides information such as the keyword density that a particular search engine is using in order for you to obtain a top listing, and places where you should (or should not) be using your keywords.

Meta description

Going back to the example of the HTML source code from our website, if you look at the first few lines you will see:

```
<html>
<head>
<title>Websurfer Netcafe website positioning
promotion ranking techniques tips tricks and how
to's</title>
<meta name="description" content="Websurfer Netcafe,
your marketing resource location for website
promotion">
<meta name="keywords" content="websurfer netcafe website
promotion positioning placement website search
engine positioning positioning optimization
ranking resource services training techniques
marketing free advertising analysis consulting">
</head>
```

The meta description tag in bold is the HTML tag that many of the search engines use to display your listing in their database.

For instance, if you go to http://www.excite.com and do a search on 'website positioning' (without the quotes), our site http://www.websurfer-netcafe.com is listed number one at the time of writing. If you go to our site and view the source code, then look at the <meta name="description" content=""> tag and then compare it to the description that is listed on www.excite.com, you will notice that they are identical to the point where Excite truncates the text to fit their format.

This is why it is important to include the meta description tag in all of your web pages.

Furthermore, you will want to develop a meta description that includes your keywords and will catch the viewer's eye and make them want to visit your site. For example, on our site http://www.websurfer-netcafe.com, we offer search engine placement services, consulting and self-study guides. Currently our meta description tag looks like this:

```
<meta name="description" content="Websurfer Netcafe,
your marketing resource location for strategies
and website promotion, search engine placement,
optimization and positioning services. Free
ranking analysis of your site">
```

However, by the time this book is published, it will probably have been changed depending on the results we achieve. This is something that you (like us) have to experiment with regularly so as to find what yields the best results.

Our advice is to keep the meta tag short. You will no doubt recall all the website descriptions that end suddenly when you are reading them from the search engine/directory results returned. Overall you have between 12 and 20 words to play with.

Remember that the world of optimization is a constantly changing one. We have to review and recalibrate our site optimization programming continually to remain at the forefront of our own highly competitive market.

Meta keyword

This is one of the most commonly abused HTML tags. Many of the search engines have actually started penalizing websites for their improper use of this tag. Previously many webmasters used a technique referred to as 'keyword stuffing', meaning taking your keyword or keywords and repeating them numerous times within the meta keyword tag.

Here is an example with a keyword that we would target if we were attempting keyword/phrase stuffing:

```
<meta name="keyword" content="website positioning,
website positioning, website positioning, website
positioning, website positioning, website
positioning, website positioning, website
positioning, website positioning, website
positioning, website positioning, website
positioning, website positioning, website
positioning, website positioning, website
positioning">
```

This technique worked for a while until the search engine technology teams caught on. Today it will get your entire site permanently banned from many of the search engines.

You can still use the meta keywords tag within an optimization tactic as there are some search engines that continue to use this tag to determine the relevancy of your site. However, you have to be sure not to duplicate your keywords too often.

When designing your meta keywords tag, don't forget to include misspellings of your words. For example, website positioning might be spelled *webstie* or *wbesite* or *postioning* etc. What this will do is win you additional traffic from those who misspell the words in their haste to enter them into the search field at their favourite search engine/directory.

Comment tag

The comment tag is an area that spidering search engines will use to index the text. However, nowadays, this area is being construed as a spamming technique and we do not recommend using it. However, if you end up needing to use it this is what is would look like:

```
<!--place your comments (keywords) here-->
```

This tag usually goes at the top of your page between the <html> and the <head> tags, like this:

```
<html>
<!--comment tag-->
<head>
<title>
<meta name="description" content="write your web pages
description here">
<meta name="keywords" content="your keywords">
</head>
```

Heading tags

The <h1></h1> or heading tags make the text on your web page appear as **bold** text instead of standard or normal type. It is advantageous to use the heading

HTML tags instead of the BOLD command due to the fact that search engines place more importance on the heading tag. The theory is similar to the format used in a newspaper.

For example, most people tend to scan the headlines to find something that catches their eye and then they read the article. Search engines function in a similar manner: they spider your web page and place more importance on the heading than they would if the text used a larger font or the BOLD command.

You would use the heading tag and place your important keywords within the heading as a further means of enhancing your website's position.

Body tags

This is where you will place the majority of your text. Ensure that you use correct spelling (grammatical rules including punctuation apply) as this is what a prospective customer will actually read when they visit your website's home page.

Bear in mind that when you write your paragraphs you will want to use your primary keywords near the beginning of the body, a few times throughout, and at the end of your copy. (Take a look at LuxuryTies.com's home page.) Depending on the search engine you should use your keywords/key phrases between three and five times throughout your home page's body copy.

For specific details as to the most current combination that a search engine will want to see in order to enable you to achieve the highest ranking(s) you should subscribe to the reporting service 'The Unfair Advantage Book on Winning the Search Engine Wars' (again you can find a link on our site).

ALT image tag

```
<img name="title" src="images/title.gif" alt="Place your
keywords here" border="0" width="680" height="157">
```

The ALT image tag was designed to accommodate older browsers and slower internet connections that wouldn't load graphics (or show where the graphic would be if it could be seen by those slower internet connections). For example, if you hovered your mouse over where the graphic was supposed to appear a box would be displayed with words in the ALT tag. (When the graphic doesn't appear you generally see an outline or frame of where the graphic was and a small cross or three-coloured propeller blade, indicating that your computer couldn't load it.)

Search engines, however, will index the text written in an ALT tag and therefore it makes sense to place your keywords there and even name your graphic after your keywords.

Make sure that you research the specific search engine you are targeting and that you do not exceed the keyword density of that search engine when designing your web pages.

Hyperlink URL tag

The hyperlink URL would look like this: http://www.websurfer-netcafe.com. There are a couple of different ways to include your keywords in the hyperlink URL.

- *Example 1.* You can build doorway pages named after your keywords. If your keyword/key phrase is 'search engine promotion' then you would name the page search-engine-promotion.html, search_engine_promotion. html, searchenginepromotion.html, etc. This would give you a hyperlink like this:

  - http://www.websurfer-netcafe.com/search_engine_promotion.html

  - http://www.websurfer-netcafe.com/search_engine_promotion.html

  - http://websurfer-netcafe.com/searchenginepromotion.html

- *Example 2.* You can register a domain name with your keywords in the domain name itself like this:

  - http://www.search-engine-promotion-services.com

Hyperlink text

The hyperlink keyword text is the text that someone visiting your website would actually see, eg find more on **search engine promotion** software at Search Engine Promotion Services. In this example, the phrase 'search engine promotion' is the link text. The actual hyperlink may look like this:

http://www.websurfer-netcafe.com/search-engine-promotion.html

or like this:

http://www.search-engine-promotion-services.com

The first example uses keywords in the hyperlink URL by naming a doorway page after your keywords/key phrases. The second example uses keywords in the hyperlink URL by acquiring a domain name with your keywords in the domain name itself.

It has been stated that many search engines will place more importance on the top-level domain name(s) as shown in the second example, and we suggest that you acquire domain names with your keywords in them.

CHAPTER 14

Search engine optimization techniques

In order to learn how to beat your competitors, you must understand some of the techniques that they could be employing which may be contrary to ethical optimization tactics.

Please note (and here's the disclaimer) that the use of these techniques can result in your entire domain (website) being banned permanently from one or more of the major search engines.

We are simply detailing the ones we know of so as to make you aware of what is being used. We do *not* provide any endorsement of these techniques, nor will we take responsibility for their use (our lawyers told us to add that!).

Keyword stuffing

We *most definitely do not* recommend using this technique. We only mention it so that you are aware of it and understand what it is. Let it be known that, if caught, the use of this technique will result in your entire domain being banned.

There really isn't a specific place in which this technique is used, as it can be deployed in any of the HTML tags and with any combination of techniques. For example, one of the most common places that keyword stuffing is used is in the <meta name="keyword" content="keyword,keyword,keyword,">. But it can also be used in the title tags, the meta description, the body, etc.

Redirects

Redirects can be employed in a legitimate manner. If a page is no longer available for whatever reason a redirect could be used to send visitors to the new home page or main index page of the website to which it now belongs.

For example, if you went to http://www.websurfer-netcafe.com/WIDGETS.html and the page was no longer available because we had stopped selling widgets I could use a redirect to send you to http://www.websurfer-netcafe.com.

Just because we stopped selling widgets doesn't mean I don't want you visiting my site and looking around, so sending you to the home page is like a second chance for me to make a sale.

The opposite would be if the visitor gets 'Page Not Found Error' and, because of this, returns to the search results and then selects a competitor's website.

When redirects are employed in this manner, it is deemed as acceptable. However, there are many people who like to use this technique in a negative manner, where they optimize web pages to rank high under keywords/key phrases that are totally different from what the website is about – think back to the 'Hunters Ties' search and all those adult content and gambling related sites.

That form of redirect misuse would *not* be acceptable and most search engines and directories will drop your web page (if not your entire site) if you are caught using redirects in such a manner.

There are different forms of redirects. One you can use legitimately is meta refresh, which is the most common and also the most easily detected:

```
<html>
<head>
<title>your web page title</title>
<META http-equiv="Refresh" content="0;
URL=http://www.whatever-site.com">
</head>
```

You can determine the time it takes for the page to refresh by setting the value of the content="any number". This equals the number of seconds before the viewer is redirected to the site specified within the meta refresh tag.

You can redirect using scripts such as:

```
<script language="javascript">
window.location.href="http://yourwebpage.com/";
//-->
</script>
```

Single pixel gifs

This technique involves the use of a single pixel gif (a gif is a picture or image file setting) hyperlinked to your doorway pages. Some search engines only want you to submit your main index.html or home page and will ignore all submissions from sub-level domains or URLs that point to a specific page other than your index page.

Their theory is that their spider will follow the links from your home page to the rest of your website's pages … Now, if we have this clear, you spend valuable time optimizing doorway pages that focus on the specific products or services you are marketing and you can't even submit them so that a search engine will index and include them in their database. So if you can only submit your home page, how do you get your doorway pages listed in the search engines?

Easy! You open up your graphics software (normally Adobe), choose *New* and set the dimensions of your graphic to 1 pixel by 1 pixel. Then find the settings for the *effects* and make it *transparent*.

Because the graphic is so small and transparent visitors to your website can't see it, but when a search engine spiders your page it will see the hyperlink from it to your doorway page.

You can place several of these single pixel graphics on your page or you can build what we call a hallway page. A hallway page is nothing more than a links page: the search engine spider follows the single pixel graphic hyperlink to the links page and then all of those links to their pages and so on.

You can take this technique to its next logical stage. If you go back to the section where we described the different HTML tags and places where you can apply your keywords/key phrases (the section where we discussed ALT tags), then this technique becomes twice as effective.

Below is an example of what the tag should look like in actual HTML format:

```
<p><img border="0" src="images/single-pixel-graphic.gif" Alt="
Keyword,keyword, keyword, keyword" width="1"
height="1"></p>
```

You specify the location of the graphic via the 'src' section of the tag, meaning you list the folder that you keep your graphics in on your server and then the name of the graphic separated with the forward slash (/) key.

Ol' switcheroo

This particular technique falls into the same category as keyword stuffing and using redirects to mislead people in order to boost your traffic. We in no way endorse this technique and again we only list it for your information so that you are aware of the methods in use – but not by us, of course!

The actual process involves building a doorway or entrance page optimized to a specific keyword/key phrase and thereafter submitting it to, and hopefully getting it listed high in, the search engines. Once this is done you replace it on your server with another page with the same name but with content that is totally different from the page a visitor will have clicked on.

Another type/form of this involves the use of the technique called 'redirect', where a page is built and optimized to achieve a high ranking under a particular keyword/key phrase. After the page has been indexed and accepted, the webmaster edits the page with a redirect and the unsuspecting viewer is sent to a different web page, with (in many cases) alternative content.

This is a fairly common and rather old technique. The main problem with it – aside from any ethical consideration – is that the next time the search engine comes through to spider your website it will usually get dropped from its current position. In the event that you get caught using these techniques, you stand a good chance of getting your website blacklisted from the many quality search engines.

Using images to your advantage

Images are great to look at – they spruce up a web page and with today's animation capabilities (and faster internet connectivity) real flair can be added to websites.

However, graphics have a tendency to increase page download times and cannot be indexed by search engines since search engines themselves place more importance on the text closest to the top. Therefore it makes sense to put text at the top of a page and not graphics.

When you have graphics at the very top of your web page, it pushes the text further down, losing points. Search engine optimization is like a game – the one with the highest score wins first place and since most webmasters don't understand search engine optimization, they usually place graphics at the top of their web pages. If this is the case, there is a way in which you can help combat the negative effect.

Looking back at the section on HTML tags again, referring to the <img alt> tag, be sure to include your most important keywords there when you have graphics at the top of your web page.

To take this a step further you can name your graphics after your keywords/key phrases. For instance, if your key phrase is 'search engine promotion' then name your graphic 'search-engine-promotion.gif'.

ASCII hierarchy

The ASCII hierarchy is the numerical/alphabetical order in which some engines and directories list websites.

When designing websites for directories, it's a good idea to use the ASCII hierarchy technique to gain an advantage over others who are not aware of these technical issues.

A good example of a site using this technique is #1 Search Engine Ranking Services, located at http://www.search-engine-ranking-services.com. Notice that both the title of the site and the name of the site match.

This is extremely important if you plan to implement this technique, as most directories that use this type of sorting method have human editors and are aware that such techniques are used to gain leverage and achieve higher rankings.

Another good example is 'Affordable Website Promotion' located at http://www.affordable-website-promotion.com. Again note that the name of the website, the title of the website and the domain name/URL all match in order to substantiate the technique.

If your site name is 'Zac's Auto Parts' and you try to use a title like 'A1 Auto Parts' or something that doesn't closely match, chances are you may get penalized. Now, if your name is Zac and you are marketing auto parts, you may want to play with the name of your site before you register a domain name.

You might want to name your site something like ' Auto Parts by Zac' – use your imagination and don't rush through these decisions as a little extra time spent on creative thinking can make all the difference. For your information, here is the ASCII hierarchy:

! " # $ % & ' ( ) * + , – . / 0 1 2 3 4 5 6 7 8 9 : ; < = > ? @ A B C D E F G H I J K L M N O P Q R S T U V W X Y Z ` a b c d e f g h I j k l m n o p q r s t u v w x y z.

You will notice that the third symbol in the ASCII hierarchy is '#' (pound or hash sign). Referring back to the site that we mentioned '#1 Search Engine Ranking Services', using the # symbol in the name of the site itself along with the title of the site allows us to employ this technique without incurring any penalties from the directories and search engines that we are attempting to gain a high listing/ranking on.

So now, go back to the website http://www.search-engine-ranking-services.com and look at the title and name of the website. Also go to http://www.msn.com or to http://www.looksmart.com and search under the key phrase 'search engine ranking' and you will notice that the website http://www.search-engine-ranking-services.com is listed number one in MSN and number two in Looksmart (at the time of writing).

Using the '#' sign in our title and site name gives us a boost on the search engines and directories that still use the ASCII hierarchy.

Comment tag

The comment tag in actual HTML format looks like this:

```
"<--place your keywords here-->"
```

The text within the comment tag is not displayed anywhere on the web page and can only be seen when viewing the source code of the web page itself.

As with other search engine optimization techniques, excessive use of this method on any web page may result in the website being penalized for spamming. Usually the comment tag is deployed at the top of a web page to gain an extra boost because of the increased importance that search engines place on text closest to the top.

Invisible text

Actually the text isn't invisible – it is usually the same colour or extremely close to the colour of the background. (An example is if the background is white and the text colour is also white.)

This will allow the page to contain more text than usual (a benefit for some engines), but visitors will not be able to see or read the text due to the fact that it is the same colour as the background.

This technique is usually combined with the another technique referred to as 'spamdexing' or 'keyword stuffing'.

There are ways around this without setting off the spam radar:

• When you look at the actual HTML code that makes up a web page, colours are specified by a series of numbers or letters (or any combination). For example '000000' (the number 0, not the letter O)is the colour code for black, whereas 'FFFFFF' equals white.

• As long as the colour code for the background and the colour code for the text are far enough apart to appear different to the search engines, yet to the human eye they are so close that there isn't any noticeable difference, you may be able to sneak it past. (But beware – most of the search engines heavily penalize web pages that use this technique if discovered, and you may even get your entire site banned as well. Therefore we do not recommend this approach.)

Hidden links

Hidden links are commonly used in conjunction with the 'single pixel gif' trick previously covered but there are other ways to employ this technique.

You can link punctuation differently from the rest of the text. For example, in the link text that you see on the web page 'Search Engine Promotion Services', this is the actual HTML code for the hyperlink:

```
<p><a href="http://www.search-engine-promotion-
services.com">Search Engine Promotion Services</a><a
href="http://www.
searchengine-positioning-services.com">.</a></p>
```

As you can see from the second hyperlink in the previous example, the text that is shown is nothing more than the period (full stop) at the end of the phrase.

The words 'search engine promotion services' link to http://www.search-engine-promotion-services.com and the period (full stop) at the end of the phrase links to http://www.searchengine-positioning-services.com – two entirely different websites (99.9% of the people will place their mouse pointer in the middle of the link and click). This would be the site that you want people to visit.

The purpose of linking punctuation is so that there are links on your page for the search engines to follow when spidering your site without having to worry about visitors finding those pages unexpectedly.

Now, depending on the other techniques and strategies that you are implementing this would determine whether or not you want these links to be visible. By this we mean that some engines use what is called link popularity to rank your pages, and having these hidden links to pages on other websites can help boost the link popularity for your own website without having your visitor bounce around from site to site.

Plurals and misspellings

Anticipating plurals and misspellings is another way to win increased traffic without jeopardizing your site and getting banned for using spam techniques.

For instance, if your key phrase is 'search engine positioning', you might want to include "**sae**rch engine positioning", "search engine po**sti**oning", etc.

Use misspellings in all areas of your web page except in the browser/site visitor text: if a prospective customer notices that you cannot spell it may impact on their purchase decision – and, let's face it, with all the competition out there we can't afford to take chances on losing prospective customers/clients on account of sloppy work.

However, using the most common misspellings in some of your keywords/ key phrases will increase your site traffic and may win you that extra customer. Moreover, you are not misleading anyone and are not using unethical methods of promotion.

The use of plurals is yet another way to win additional site traffic. If you are focusing on the key phrase 'search engine ranking service**s**', you can be found under the key phrase 'search engine ranking service' as well.

However, if you focus on 'search engine ranking service' it's not likely that you would be found under 'search engine ranking service**s**'. The reason behind this is that many search engines are using a technique called 'word stemming'.

This means that you can get 'service' out of 'service**s**' or 'printer' out of 'printer**s**' as the search engine can determine the non plural form of the word, but it cannot make words plural. Therefore using plurals can prove to be a great advantage.

This is a brief summary of the most common techniques and tricks that are used. Obviously there are many (and we mean thousands) more out there but most of these are less frequently used so we have not described them here.

CHAPTER 15

Being more productive: automating your tasks

Regardless of whether you're a new start-up business or a Fortune 500, time is money. The more efficiently you can work and the more productive you are, the more profitable your website/company will be, but to be more productive you will need to cover more ground in less time.

There are a couple of different ways in which you can overcome the 'no time for anything like this' obstacle, as we fully agree that the whole e-marketing and optimization process is time consuming:

- You can increase your administrative staff. Of course you would have to pay them and train them to be self-sufficient, which can take weeks, even months, and then you have the possibility that they will still make a mistake or miss something that will get your site penalized or banned from the search engines.

- Alternatively you could automate your tasks with the help of software. We have compiled a list with some explanation of the software that we have found to be the most useful, easy to understand and very user friendly.

What is the first thing that you really need to know with any optimization function? For us it has always been where the website currently ranks, and what optimization work has previously been conducted on it.

If you end up submitting the website to a search engine and (without your prior knowledge) someone else has recently submitted it to that same search engine, you could get penalized for spam as the website has been submitted to the same engine too often without any significant changes. It is always best to keep some form of website optimization history to review when designing a new promotional/technical-based campaign.

Moreover, if you try to optimize an already highly ranked web page you could actually decrease its ranking instead of increasing it. After all, we are talking about being efficient here, and it pays to take note of the old maxim 'if it ain't broke don't mend it!' We suggest therefore that before you start rearranging your programming you take a good look at where your site currently is in the search engines and directories. It may be a case of leaving well alone if you are satisfied with the results you are achieving through your existing ranking.

Now in order to determine where you currently rank you can go to each search engine and type in your keyword/key phrase and then scroll through the results to see if and where you are listed under that keyword. However, this doesn't sound very efficient. How long would it take you to search each of the top 10–15 search engines for each of your 10, 20, 50 100… keywords?

Well, let's try and estimate. Even with a high-speed internet connection, we estimate that on average it takes about 30 seconds from typing in a 2–3-word key phrase and clicking search to obtain a list of results that you still need to sort through.

We always start by viewing the top 100 results only. By the time you scroll through all 100 results you have spent anywhere between 5 and 10 minutes.

So you take 5 minutes per key phrase, per search engine. Even if you only searched on the top 10 engines and directories using 100 keywords – which isn't really a lot even for a small company – it would take you 83.3 hours to determine where your website ranks. And what if your company operates more than one website?

Now you can get some idea as to why this has to be an automated task! (You can find additional information regarding the following named software at http://www.websurfer-netcafe.com.)

WebPosition Gold

One of the software programs that we use extensively for this particular function is called WebPosition Gold. You can locate a link at http://www.websurfer-netcafe.com where you will find more information along with pricing and ordering details if you are interested in purchasing the software (and any other software we recommend here).

WebPosition Gold (WPG) is a multitasked software package. The main reason that we use it is for the website URL reporter function, which tells you where your site is listed in relation to your keywords/key phrases.

You can set up the software to scan any combination of the top 15 or so search engines that it supports (it updates and adds more on a regular basis), stipulating how many searches to scan per search engine and for which keywords/key phrases to conduct the multiple searches.

After you have set the variables, you can click on start and off it goes! Depending on your internet connection, the number of keywords/key phrases that you are searching on, the number of engines that are being searched along with how many results you are searching through, this process can take a couple of hours to run. However, two, maybe even three hours is a whole lot better that 83.3.

The good part is that WPG has a feature called 'Scheduler' where you can set the software to run on its own at any time day or night. So that while you are away from the office, at home watching television or even fast asleep this software can be at work performing these very time-consuming and complex tasks which are vitally important to you in your website optimization programme.

The software contains additional functions such as a web 'Page Generator' and a web 'Page Critic'. Web Page Generator is a template style option that builds doorway pages for you. All you have to do is fill in a few fields and click start and Page Generator completes all the HTML code for you. Although you should exercise caution when using Page Generator as many search engines have developed filters that will drop web pages that appear to be similar in size, content and topic.

Then the web 'Page Critic' function activates and analyzes the *code* of the page that was just created and displays the areas that we addressed previously in order to match what the search engine wants to see.

WebPosition Gold also has a home page submitter feature that you can use to submit your site to the search engines that it supports and an inbuilt tracking function. The tracking function actually installs a little programming script on your web page and when someone visits it, the script logs all the information such as the referring URL (where the visitor came from), what search phrase they used to find your website, if they came from a search engine, and so on.

Armed with this information, you can determine which keywords/key phrases are working and which aren't, make any necessary adjustments and then resubmit your pages to the engines in a bid to improve the website's overall ranking.

A word of caution: when using the reporter function, bear in mind that excessive use may have repercussions. For example, Google has been known to block IP addresses (basically the phone number) of the computers running automated searches of its database.

Due to the time it takes for most search engines to update and refresh their index, running reports weekly should prove to be more than enough. And to be even safer, use the scheduler feature to run the reports during off-peak hours.

GRSeo (GR Search Engine Optimizer)

Some of the features contained within the WebPosition Gold software overlap with those of GRSeo. However, GRSeo has certain capabilities that WebPosition Gold does not and these additional resources alone are extremely useful.

One theory that we have always relied on is that a second opinion never hurts and if that's true a third can only be better. Well, GRSeo is the second opinion (or WebPosition Gold would be the second opinion if you use GRSeo first!). Either way, GRSeo's primary objective is to analyze your web pages and point out areas that can cause you penalties on submission or indexing of your website.

The resources that the software draws from are updated monthly so it stays on top of regular changes in all the search engines/directories.

Swiss Army Applications for Webmasters

We use this software as a third opinion. It will take a snapshot of your web page and display what the search engine sees, giving you two looks that vary slightly. What we most like about this software is the format it uses to display results, as it gives a concise view of what a search engine actually sees.

Really it's like being given the ability to test your work on a search engine without having to learn by your mistakes. This software provides you with a view that you can't see with other forms of software, and also contains features from tracking affiliate programs to a full suite of search engine submission features.

GRKda (GR Keyword Density Analyzer)

This is what we would consider to be one of the most important and time-saving programs available.

Search engines base their ranking algorithms on the keyword density to determine what your web page is about. To recap, for example, let's say your keyword is 'computer'. If you have 100 words on your web page and you use 'computer' five times, your keyword density would be 5%.

However, what if you are using a two- or even three-word key phrase, eg 'search engine promotion'? You have to look at the level of word density for each word in the phrase and calculate the density of the entire phrase *meaning that the density of each word can vary from the density of the entire phrase*. Let us expand further on this point.

Throughout your web page, as you fill in the body content and talk about your product or service (in this illustration we will use 'search engine promotion' as the phrase in question), every occurrence of any word in the key phrase will count and increase the density.

During the description and explanation of 'search engine promotion' we may use a sentence like this 'Go to AltaVista and search on your key phrase'. Notice how we used the word 'search' – that will count towards the word density or percentage of times that the word is used.

If you use any of the words that are in your key phrase anywhere else it can throw out your calculations. If the density is too high, then the search engine may determine that the word 'search' is more of a filler word such as 'and' or 'the'. If the keyword density isn't high enough, the search engine may determine that your web page is about something entirely different.

As you can imagine this could be a serious problem. So what can you do about it? GRKda – GR Keyword Density Analyzer – is a great asset and time-saver for learning and defining the word density calculations. You can also analyze your competitors' web pages in a matter of minutes to determine their keyword densities and adjust yours to beat them!

WebPosition Gold will tell you what the top scoring pages' average for keyword density is, its placement and so on. But 'average' and 'precise' can mean the difference between a top 20 or a top 10 position, and when you are working within an extremely competitive business landscape you need every advantage you can get. So it pays to check, keep records and be highly organized in your choice and calibration of keywords, phrases and placements.

Inexpensive Cloaking Script

Cloaking – also known as 'stealth techniques' – can be deployed in both an ethical and non-ethical manner.

Cloaking is a method used to determine whether the visitor to your website is a search engine spider or an actual human visitor. What's the advantage in this? Well, people like to see flashy, interactive web pages but all of the technology used to make these web pages, eg Java, Flash, graphics, etc will lower your rankings as search engines cannot index them. Cloaking allows you to build different web pages specifically designed for search engines and for people. The cloaking script itself determines whether the visitor is a search engine or a human. If the visitor is a search engine spider, then a page that is specifically designed for that particular search engine is served and indexed; alternatively if it is a human visitor, then the page designed for humans is displayed.

So, the advantage is that you can build the nice flashy pages for your prospective customers while optimizing pages to rank highly in the search engines without the flash graphics etc.

Caution must be exercised when using this technique as many unethical webmasters use the approach to optimize pages for search engines to achieve high rankings for a certain keyword or phrase, while the page that the human visitor sees is entirely different – remember our earlier example of 'ties' taking you to a gambling content site. Using cloaking or stealth techniques in this manner *will* get your entire site banned if you are caught.

There's a lot of controversy regarding cloaking and whether or not it should in fact be used. For your information, we use it on all of our sites. However, we use it ethically, meaning the only difference between the pages that a search engine sees and the pages that human visitors see is a matter of graphics, frames, etc. The actual text contained on the search engine pages is the same text that appears on the visitor pages. The main difference is that the search engine pages are nothing but text whereas the human pages have pictures and so on. Therefore, there is nothing on the page that could lower its score and affect its ranking within the engines.

We use a cloaking script called 'Inexpensive Cloaking Script'. You can find more information about this software at http://www.websurfer-netcafe.com. It allows you to optimize your pages independently for many of the major search engines as well as allowing you to specify a page for generic search engines. Inexpensive Cloaking Script is (as its name suggests) an inexpensive program that's also very easy to use.

Again, we must mention that cloaking can be considered a spam technique by many search engines. We do not endorse this technique nor will we accept any responsibility for its use, but it can be used in an ethical way.

Summary

You should by now, have a good idea of what optimization is all about. More importantly, you should be able to take a good look at your own website and start making any necessary adjustments to begin your own optimization project.

As stated throughout the previous chapters, there are plenty of additional resources located at the website http://www.websurfer-netcafe.com which will provide the further information you need and links to other software you can use. Many organizations actually give free trials so you can test the programs before you purchase, just as we did.

The authors both agree that there will be even more solutions to website marketing and the creation of on-line brands as the internet itself develops further. Our message to you is to try out this process for yourself. If you can understand and apply the basics you'll soon be able to move into the advanced processes of invisible script and single pixel gifs – it's good fun, and if you enjoy the challenge it won't feel like a chore.

CHAPTER 16

Optimizing a home page to meet a niche market

We are now going to put the previous chapters into practice by creating a fully optimized home page and website search engine marketing programme for LuxuryTies.com, aimed at the MBA tie-wearing market segment identified earlier.

By following this example you will see how to apply what you have learned throughout this book to your own e-business. The result will be a highly ranked home page that is tuned to the specific terms and phrases your market uses when looking for the type of products/services you have on offer.

Setting the optimization framework

Having undertaken our brief research into our target market, Hunters (as the controlling website organization or webmaster) has decided to target the two million existing MBAs and the 90,000 graduating each year. We will be honouring their qualification with an 'unofficial' necktie design (you may in your case be using different information or a tangible product), and we will optimize LuxuryTies.com to engage this new market.

The type of message we want to get over quickly falls into two parts:

- We need to tell people what we have and why it's unique to them.

- We need to deliver our credentials and elements of the value-added experience they will gain from using our site.

We will employ some old off-line sales techniques to engage the market, while ensuring that we do not trade down the qualification or belittle anyone (remember customers aren't fools so don't treat them as if they are). We will attempt to speak to the market using some of its own language, which should enthuse the segment enough to enter and view the range – and ultimately buy a Hunters' MBA design tie.

In creating the new home page let's take a look back at our own thoughts as shown in Figure 16.1.

 Content and Display

* Use alternative display – pictures (JPEGs) reduce words

* Make it slick, avoid humour, watch download times

* Look at competitor graduation gift(s)

* Provoke thought in first few words

* Avoid harsh colours – keep the tone soft

* Create a separate MBA site marketing programme

Figure 16.1 Home page criteria.

The home page design

We have to employ the phrases and terms that our new target market uses to search under within our home page content and the HTML programming tags behind the home page itself.

We realize that some search engines and directories index manually by only reading the home page, not taking into account any of the programming. This means that we have to focus our text/content on:

- a succinct home page message that will interest the market

- ensuring our content/text is relevant to what we are offering so that we are indexed in the correct category (more on this later).

In this way we will meet the criteria of the search engines and directories with manual indexing protocols, while catering for the others whose indexing process is automated, triggered by the programming behind the home page, when we submit or re-submit our URL www.LuxuryTies.com.

That said, clearly the most important words, terms and phrases for this market are:

Term	GoTo search term frequency results
MBA	20,785
Master of Business Administration	553
Graduation gifts	4,817
Ties	15,134
Neckties	9,279
Savile Row	555
Alumni	17,291

As in Part 2, in order to find these popular words/terms that our segment employs we simply perform a search on a number of search engines/directories and use the GoTo search analysis tool at www.payperclicktools.com.

It should be noted that no one ever searches specifically under the phrase 'MBA ties', and therefore we won't have that within our programming. Just because we sell them it doesn't mean people know how to ask for them, especially as we cannot afford to advertise the fact that we are offering a unique MBA tie to generate a market interest that might not be there.

You have to remember when you are constructing keywords/phrases that you must think as the searcher would, employing only the words/phrases that contain the generic term (ties, graduation gifts, etc) in the programming element behind the home page and then include the words/phrases on the home page itself. By this we mean mixing generic terms such as 'MBA' and 'ties' together.

For example, we can mix the term 'graduation gifts' with 'MBA' – and we will also mix other generic terminology to draw in those of our market who are simply surfing, checking out what's around.

The new LuxuryTies.com draft home page is shown in Figure 16.2. It's the best we can achieve: we feel it is simple to understand and will motivate our audience's thoughts in a quick and friendly manner.

MBA Executive Managers Only

'Because the best have to look the best'

Hunters, the exclusive necktie makers of London's Savile Row, know this, and to meet the requirements of our increasing number of professional MBA manager clients we have designed a unique series of Master of Business Administration stripe club ties to provide you with the elegance and style your qualification deserves for any situation, be it interview, business school alumni reunion or as a special MBA graduation gift – viewable in our interactive tie fitting room.

Click the picture right to visit the MBA tie styling cabinet at: _www.luxuryties.com_

Hunters Partnership
Savile Row's Master Silk Tie Maker
E-mail: info@luxuryties.com
Tel: 011 44 207 734 5242

Figure 16.2 Target home page for Hunters' MBA ties.

In our new home page we are going to use a picture of an MBA tie in a very low JPEG graphic image size, and add a hyperlink enabling the browser to go straight to the MBA ties on our website (note there are normally three pages including the home page before a browser gets to see our ties). We feel that it is important to speed the clicks to view process up, as this particular tie-wearing segment is fairly time-constrained and will want to get in and out quickly.

The reason for using a picture here is that we can get more over visually than we can in a thousand words, and if we use a reduced JPEG image (low pixel count) the page download time should be fairly short.

The background will continue to be the silhouette of the building, with the name label as the regular website entry button.

The use of our key (or main) target words/phrases (density) in our home page is as follows:

MBA	4
Master of Business Administration	1
Tie(s)	4
Neckties	1
Savile Row	2
Graduation gift	1
Alumni	1

Without overusing any word we can (and have) created a coherent text. You'll notice that we employ a few of the usual 'reverse marketing' techniques by stating that only those with an MBA are eligible (the premise being that anyone who is not an MBA will still take a look), and then play up to the market by stating that 'to be the best you have to look the best' .

We then go on to say that the ties are unique and can be viewed in the interactive fitting room, just to stimulate some curiosity – 'what's that all about?'.

So that's what we are going with at this stage! If we want to we can just save what we have put together in a Microsoft web page format and then forward it to our website builders who will organize this as our new home page. Ease of updating is vital – our builders certainly provide us with that – and although it will still need a bit more work by them we're happy with this as a first draft.

Background optimization programming

With our new home page opening presentation message set, we now have to turn our attention to the background HTML programming from a purely marketing point of view.

We know this background HTML programming is what some of the search engines use when we submit the home page for indexing within their directory, and the programming element will determine how the home page is going to perform to searches etc.

The three areas we tend to concentrate on are:

- meta description

- keywords

- content/description.

As Dean says:

> This is the basic starting point. The first and foremost tag that needs to be addressed is the HTML <title></title> tag. Focusing on this tag along with the other three areas will give you a good foundation to start off with.

In this section we will take you through the individual elements of optimization, enabling you to identify why certain search engines focus on, say, the title tag and don't bother with keywords. We then develop further the programming areas of the home page that are marketing-focused towards the main search engines/directories.

As stated earlier each of the search engines/directories is unique and has its own language that interprets your site's programming in alternative ways on submission and indexing.

We know we can alter the significance of some programming items to have more impact when we make our submissions. It's a matter of continually fine-tuning your home page to the search engines' and directories' requirements.

What will stay is the newly designed home page area that the browser or visitor sees (Figure 16.2), unless the density of certain words within the home page content itself (what the browser reads) does not allow us to figure highly in the rankings. In that case it's back to the drawing board – we have to start again, redefining our message to our market and better co-ordinating the key terms and phrases.

Below appears a brief (at this stage) description of the construction of the marketing-related website to search engine/directory programming elements on which we will be focusing. The need for these has been clarified and described in greater detail in previous chapters.

Title tag

This is what the searcher sees in the little blue strip above the MSN browser bar (where the functions File, Edit, View, etc are):

```
<HEAD><TITLE>MBA ties by Hunters Helps You Choose
The Right Graduation Gift Ties.</TITLE>
```

Keywords

These are the keywords/key phrases that a browser is likely to use when they are

---

searching for MBA, MBA related, graduation gifts, ties, etc. Each comma separates a word or phrase and we have ranked them in order of importance with MBA first (note we use both upper and lower case spellings):

```
<meta name="keywords" content="<meta name="keywords"
content="mba, MBA, MBA interviews, MBA gifts, gifts
for MBA graduates, executive ties, MBA ties,
neckties for MBAs, shirts and ties, silk ties,
matching shirts and ties, ties for interviews,
how to tie a tie, style, brands, designer brands,
Master of Business Administration, MBA style
support, shirt, ties, neckties, luxury ties,
father's day presents, executive gifts, men's
accessories, neck ties, presents for him, savile
row, bow ties, men's ties, luxuryties.com,
hunters, silk ties, gifts for him, men's birthday
presents, anniversary presents, formal wear,
shirts, woven ties, hunters">
```

At this stage in our optimization project Dean says:

> Hunters/LuxuryTies.com need to be careful when duplicating keywords, especially in the meta description tag. I have heard that search engines are actually starting to consider the use of this tag to be spam. Statistically, approximately 80% of internet searches use all lower case letters when entering their search word or phrase …
>
> It's best to use between 20 and 30 terms/phrases that are specific to what you do (relevancy) and not to use the same word too often, eg 'ties, ties, ties', as this may result in your home page submission being rejected.

Looking at what we have suggested above, it is clear in the light of Dean's comments that we have overused the words MBA and ties in both their upper and lower case forms, and changes will need to be made before we submit the new home page.

Description/content

This is the description of what our website is all about, used by the search engines and/or directories when presenting search results back to the browser (the website's details are returned along with a short description of what the website is about):

```
<meta name="Description" content="MBA graduation gift
ties by Hunters of Savile Row viewed only at our
interactive tie fitting room.">
```

These areas have been discussed in greater detail in Chapters 11 and 12, giving you deeper insight as to their full relevance, while Chapter 13 deals with some of the many techniques that can be employed – the tips and tricks of search engine optimization – to really move a website up the ranks.

We must admit that when we originally looked at the background HTML programming for the home page we too thought 'that looks complicated'. The fact is, it's not – you just have to learn where everything goes, what the different terms mean and how it all interacts together.

What we have demonstrated in this straightforward example is just a very basic search engine optimization and home page focused message. Your studies of the previous chapters will have shown you how far it can all be advanced.

A final example of the importance of optimization is the case of a website owner who told me they were in a number one position on a search engine. When we asked what search term they could be found under they gave us their website domain name URL as the search term to use. We didn't want to hurt their feelings, but we can all be number one for our own domain name as it is unique. However, it's worthless if no one ever uses that word, term or phrase to search for the products/service you are selling, especially if the market doesn't even know you exist.

It's the same with search terms that are obscure. Some professional website optimization consultants will extol the virtues of being number one for any search term even if it is remote, heralding it as a victory for the website and enabling them to justify their 'professional' fees! For example, LuxuryTies could easily get a number one slot for the term 'Savile Row Silk Ties', but what would be the point? No one ever uses that term to search for ties.

Remember: keep your search terms and home page specific to your target segment and the generic words and phrases it most commonly uses to find products or services like yours and you can't go wrong.

And finally …

You should now understand what's going to be needed to make your e-commerce application the success it deserves to be. Hopefully you will be approaching this with either a renewed vigour or a sense of enthusiasm, especially as a lot of the technical concepts have been demystified.

As we said at the outset, life is all about self-help – the more you can do for yourself the better placed you'll be both financially and in terms of your own personal satisfaction at having beaten the odds and created a winning formula to market your business.

Customers are the all-important factor – never lose sight of that. Whatever you do must be geared towards their enjoyment and benefit, and if you go on to create a great brand that means something to people you will have made your mark on this world of ours.

We know how tough and, sometimes, how near impossible the whole function of e-commerce (and business) can be. You have the great ideas, you have the ambition to see it through, to make it the success you yearn for, thereby silencing your critics and perhaps even making the same journey to New York as we once did.

We hope one day you'll get there, and marvel just as we did at the sights and sounds that represented for us the start of a great time in business.

However, never lose sight of your own personal goals. Enthusiasm speaks volumes, and the more optimistic you are the less likely you are to see problems.

The last message we want to leave you with is that whenever your business dealings take a turn for the worse and the horizon looks bleak, it's then and possibly only then that you will find that extra ounce of inspiration to get up off the floor and start fighting back. There's always a solution out there – you just have to focus and then take a systematic approach. You'll emerge a better person for it!

Good luck, and thank you from all of us in both London and California.

APPENDIX A

HTML

Below is an outline of HTML (hyper text mark-up language) programming code, showing the most common tags referred to when implementing search engine optimization strategies and techniques. The left column provides a generic description of what the HTML tag is and in the right column is the tag in its actual HTML format. Bear in mind that, not only is it important to know where to apply your keywords/key phrases, but also how and, in certain areas, why this is so.

We have coded this to help you distinguish between the programming elements of HTML that are standard within optimization and the text that you would insert between the HTML programming itself, as follows:

- **text in this style** is the actual HTML opening and closing tags for each programming line

- `text in this style` is where you would place your keywords/key phrases, comments, etc.

Description	Programming HTML tag
Opening HTML tag	`<html>`
Comment line	`<!--Place your keywords here-->`
Opening head tag	`<head>`
Web page title	`<title>your web page title</title>`
Meta description	`<meta name="description" content="your webpage description">`
Meta keyword	`<meta name="keywords" content="your web page keywords">`
Meta refresh tag	`<meta http-equiv="refresh" content="10">`
Closing head tag	`</head>`
Opening body tag	`<body>`
Heading tag	`<H1>Place keywords here </H1>` Place your body copy here using your keywords throughout
Hyperlink tag *Keywords in the URL*	`<a href="http://www.search-engine-promotion-services.com">` Search Engine Promotion Services`</a>`
Hyperlink tag *Keywords in the link text*	`<a href="http://www.websurfer-netcafe.com` Search Engine Promotion Services`</a>`
Closing body tag	`</body>`
Closing HTML tag	`</html>`

APPENDIX B

Glossary of optimization terms

Doorway pages   These are web pages that are built and optimized to rank highly in the search engines. Doorway pages are usually specifically focused towards a single topic or keyword/key phrase. Pages may also be known as informational topic pages, gateway pages, etc. Doorway pages are fairly small in file size, they average 300–700 words and the keywords/key phrases are used throughout. For a more exact formula on building doorway pages go to http://www.websurfer-netcafe.com/se-news.html.

Hallway pages   A hallway page is nothing more than a links page. The hallway page contains the links to all your doorway pages, informational topics pages, gateway pages and internal pages. For an example of a hallway page go to http://www.websurfer-netcafe.com/hallway-page.html.

Keyword   A keyword is a word used to describe your product or the service that you are offering. Keywords are what a search engine user will enter in the search field to find your site.

Keyword density   Keyword density is the number of times your keyword appears in your indexable text in relation to the total indexable text on your web page. For example, if you have a total of 100 words of indexable text and you have used your keyword five times you have a 'keyword density' of 5%.

Now, if you are using multiple word phrases, eg 'search engine promotion', then you have to calculate the density of each word separately and the exact phrase as well. A couple of software programs are mentioned in the text that will help you with this task – for more information go to http://www.websurfer-netcafe.com/wpg.html or http://www.websurfer-netcafe.com/kda.html.

Keyword frequency   Keyword frequency is simply the number of times you have used your keyword within the indexable text on your web page.

Keyword frequency differs from keyword density in that it refers only to how many times you have used your keyword throughout your page, whereas keyword density refers to how many times you have used your keyword in relation to how many total indexable words you have used.

Keyword prominence   Keyword prominence relates to how close to the beginning of the HTML tag you have used your keyword. We will use 'computers' for your keyword in the following examples:

- *100% keyword prominence* – using your keyword at the beginning of your tag like this:

  `<title>`**computers** `from websurfer-netcafe</title>`

- *50% keyword prominence* – using your keyword in the middle of your tag like this:

  `<title>websurfer netcafe` **computers** `sales service</title>`

- *0% keyword prominence* – using your keyword at the end of your tag like this:

  `<title>websurfer netcafe we sell` **computers**`</title>`

Spidering   A term used to describe what a search engine does in order to index your page. A search engine spider is nothing more than a software program that runs on the search engine's server and goes to the URL (website address) that was submitted.

The spider analyzes the page located at the URL and catalogues it. After this is done, when a user goes to the search engine's own home page and performs a search on a key phrase (eg 'computers'), the search engine searches its database for web pages it has spidered that contain the word(s) being used to search under.

Index

Hunters Partnership Ltd
  brand concept 67
  brand credentials, controlling
    70–2
  brand user groups 110
  brand-influencing factors 77
  constraints on 46
  goals/objectives (internet) 25–36
  market background 3
  new economy, and 4–8
  origins 8–10
  television interview 55–6
  see also Case study (Hunters);
    LuxuryTies.com
Hyper text mark-up language
  (HTML) *see* HTML (hyper text
  mark-up language)
Hyperlink text 145–6
Hyperlink URL tag 145

Images, use of 150–1, 168
'Inexpensive Cloaking Script' 162–3
Inktomi 134
Innovation 84
Inside UK Enterprises Host Status
  xvi
Interactive Interface Technology
  Protocols 31
Internet Assist 31, 32
Internet Explorer 139
Invisible text 153

Jargon barriers 24, 52
Java Window (computer language)
  17, 27, 30
JPEG (low pixel count) image 168
Junk e-mail 132–3

KDA (Keyword Density Analyzer)
  137
Key phrases 135, 136
Keyword density 177–8
Keyword frequency 136, 178
Keyword prominence 137, 178
Keyword relevancy 136
Keyword stuffing 142, 147–8
Keywords 135–7
  background optimization
    programming 170–1
  home page 170–1
  meaning 135, 177

'Land-grab' xvii, 59, 110
Level playing field xv, xvii
Lifestyle questionnaires 21–3, 30
Lists, e-mail 132–3
Logos 59–60, 61, 64
Looksmart 134
LuxuryTies.com
  added value 65
  brand development 61–2
  customer habits, matching 29–30
  generic term searches 67–8,
    69–70
  home page 105–8, 121, 168
  Hunters and 10–12, 70–2
  see also Hunters Partnership Ltd
  initial purpose 43
  marketing issues 48
  opening statements 104
  orders, location 125
  search engines, using in marketing
    55
  team leadership 67–8
Lycos 55, 134